ECUMENISM AND VATICAN II

ECUMENISM
and VATICAN II

EDITED BY
REV. CHARLES O'NEILL, S.J.

ESSAYS BY
BERNARD COOKE, S.J.
RABBI REUVEN SIEGEL
J. H. NICHOLS
REV. JOHN MEYENDORFF
FRANCIS CANAVAN, S.J.
OTTO KARRER
PIET FRANSEN, S.J.

WITH A FOREWORD BY
VINCENT T. O'KEEFE, S.J.,
PRESIDENT OF FORDHAM UNIVERSITY

THE BRUCE PUBLISHING COMPANY
MILWAUKEE

NIHIL OBSTAT:

John A. Schulien, S.T.D.
Censor librorum

IMPRIMATUR:

✠ William E. Cousins
Archbishop of Milwaukee

June 26, 1964

The *Nihil obstat* and *Imprimatur* are official declarations that a book or pamphlet is free of doctrinal or moral error. No implication is contained therein that those who have granted the *Nihil obstat* and *Imprimatur* agree with the contents, opinions, or statements expressed.

Library of Congress Catalog Card Number: 64–23892

ⓒ 1964 The Bruce Publishing Company

FOREWORD

Pope John XXIII came to the throne of St. Peter at a unique moment in the history of the Church. He succeeded in creating a new spirit inside the Church and a new image of the Church to those outside it. Pope John's approach to non-Catholics was not in the spirit of recrimination or dissension but in love and longing. Vatican Council II was set up with a triple finality: human unity and peace; Christian unity — a necessary step to that goal; and the internal renewal of the Church — a necessary step to Christian unity.

When Pope Paul VI opened the second session of the Council in September, 1963, he reasserted the purpose of the Council as inaugurated by Pope John XXIII. Pope Paul indicated the concrete steps by which the process of *aggiornamento* was to proceed. The Council's four principal aims were announced as:

1. The Church must impart to herself and to the world a new awareness of her inner nature;
2. There must be a renewal and a reform of the Church by shedding what is unworthy or defective;
3. The unity of all Christians;
4. The Church's dialogue with men of our own day.

Thus Vatican II has created a new atmosphere of urgency with respect to the unity of all Christians. It has truly opened windows locked for centuries.

The present volume represents a partial but considerable answer to the challenge flung to all of us by these two successors of St. Peter. It speaks not to souls but to man as we know him, in the complexity of his spiritual, temporal, individual, and social nature.

Reverend Vincent T. O'Keefe, S.J.
President — Fordham University

v

PREFACE

Pope John's electrifying, dynamic call for renewal of the Church and his appeal to all men of goodwill to prepare the way for Christian unity have caught the minds and hearts of men everywhere. The whole world watches with deep-felt concern the epoch-making sessions of the Council summoned by the beloved Pope John and continued by Pope Paul to tackle earnestly this challenge to the Church today. People everywhere are passionately consumed with a thirst for information about the Council, for learning more about its repercussions throughout the world and its implications for all men, Catholic, Orthodox, Protestant, Jew, whatever their belief.

Father Charles O'Neill of Fordham University sought to quench this thirst by sponsoring a series of talks about the Council and the work of Christian unity. This book is, in large measure, one result of these talks, as it proved possible for some of the lecturers to prepare more polished versions of their addresses. To round out the volume other outstanding lectures and papers were assembled from other sources. The result is a work that comes to grips in realistic fashion with the challenges facing the Church both in her task of internal renewal and in the endeavor to collaborate with all men in preparing the way for the day when "all shall be one." As such, it has a message for all who believe that God has willed to irrupt in human history, that the Spirit is at work today in the hearts of men.

This volume would not have been possible without the cooperation and friendly collaboration of many persons — the individual contributors, Father O'Neill and Fordham University, Joseph Cunneen of *Cross Currents,* and Sister M. Julie, secretary for the Society of Catholic College Teachers. It is a pleasant duty to thank all for their much needed help.

NOTES ON CONTRIBUTORS

Rev. Bernard Cooke, S.J. — Chairman of the Department of Theology at Marquette University and past president of the Society of Catholic College Teachers of Sacred Doctrine, Father Cooke has long been active in ecumenical dialogue and has contributed to such journals as *Continuum, The Commonweal,* and *America.*

Rabbi Reuven Siegel — Rabbi of Temple Adath Israel in the Bronx, Rabbi Siegel was a Marine Chaplain during the Korean War. Clergy Co-Chairman of the National Conference of Christians and Jews and a member of the Mayor's Committee on Youth, he is in the forefront of those seeking to relate the Judaeo-Christian heritage to the American scene.

J. H. Nichols — Professor in the Divinity College of Princeton, Dr. Nichols, a Presbyterian, was an observer at the first session of the Council.

Rev. John Meyendorff — Professor of Theology at St. Vladimir's Orthodox Seminary, Father Meyendorff is a widely respected authority on the Greek Fathers and is a frequent participant in panels discussing the problems facing the unity of Christians.

Rev. Francis Canavan, S.J. — Father Canavan is an associate editor of the weekly Catholic magazine, *America.*

Rev. Walter J. Burghardt, S.J. — Father Burghardt, professor of Patristic Theology at Woodstock College, is one of the greatest authorities in the United States on the question of tradition.

Rev. Otto Karrer — Father Karrer is an eminent German theologian, best known in this country for his *The Religions of Mankind.*

Rev. Piet Fransen, S.J. — A Dutch Jesuit, Father Fransen is known to many in this country through his contributions to *Worship* and *Cross Currents.*

Rev. Charles O'Neill, S.J. (*ed.*) — Dean of Fordham's School of General Studies, Father O'Neill was a Navy Chaplain during World War II. His concern to make a university a dynamic factor in the community is reflected in the adult lecture courses sponsored by him.

CONTENTS

xi

Contents

ECUMENISM AND VATICAN II

BERNARD COOKE, S.J.

THE TASK OF ECUMENICITY*

We are witnessing, in the sessions of the Second Vatican Council, one of the key events of our twentieth century. While it is a bit presumptuous to predict the results of the council, it seems quite clear from the statements both of Popes John and Paul and of the Fathers at the Council, that two tasks are of crucial importance for the Church today: that of working seriously toward the re-union of Christians, and that of bringing the expression of the Church's life more closely into contact with our contemporary world. Achievement of these two objectives in the practical order, on the grass-roots level of men's faith and lives, depends greatly on Christian parents and educators whose God-given vocation it is to help shape the religious insights and attitudes of tomorrow's youth.

To begin with the hope of Pope John that the expression of the Church may be effectively meaningful for the men of our day: We must, I believe, insist with Genesis that the world is good, and that man is good; more than that, that man is meant to master this world, to bring it under subjection. We must then go an important step forward and teach the kingship of Christ, the fact that his dominion over all creation makes that creation good in a transcendent fashion that is only gradually being fulfilled in the course of human history. This insistence can help cut through the strange paradox of contemporary thought: a thought that is imbued with hope in mankind's inventiveness,

---

* Reprinted with permission from the 1962 *Proceedings* of the Society of Catholic College Teachers of Sacred Doctrine.

that looks to the conquest of the heavens by human exploration, that is caught up in the accelerating human understanding of material and even spiritual being; and yet a thought that is baffled before the apparent lack of any ultimate meaning to life, a thought that so often finds expression in a black nihilism, and that finds itself so inadequate in the presence of common human experience of freedom and love and death. To the men who think this way the Church must teach that all which is has great goodness and meaning, but that this goodness and meaning are grounded not in man but in God the Father and in his gift to us of his incarnated Son.

Second, we must witness in our contemporary world to a savior who is Christ, the Lord. Or, to put it another way, we must explain and live the true mystery of that redemption which is being accomplished by the death and resurrection of Jesus. As we know, the Incarnation of the Word of God is not a static reality, it is finalistically ordered to the redemption of mankind; and we also know that redemption is a process much deeper than the payment of the legal penalty of man's sinfulness. Incarnation and redemption mean the radical transformation of the being and the significance of man, his world, and his history; they mean Christianization in the full import of that term. All is to bear the mark of Christ's love; this is the judgment of the world.

Somehow we must find the way of bringing ourselves and our charges to a realistic understanding of this earth-shaking truth. We must see the risen Christ at work in and through the mystery of his Church, imparting to men that life-giving Spirit whom he sends from his Father. We must bear out into our world the humbling truth that man is utterly lost without such a savior and the consoling truth that such a savior exists.

Moreover, we must make every effort to see the reality of this redemption operative in the men and structures of our day. Ours is the task to challenge the breathtaking opportunities of our times, to build a world worthy of man who is a son of God, to translate the vision of faith into society and culture. We must be ready to show to a searching but cynical world that the answer of a suffering and risen Messiah is neither stumbling block nor foolishness but wisdom and power.

Third, the Church must validate and complement the symbolisms of our contemporary world, those symbolisms that so deeply influence men's judgments and action. This is a profound and difficult task, but one for which the very nature of the Church fits her, for she is the great Sacrament of Christ and finds expression of her life in sacramental action. Not only that, but the sacramentality of the Church is truly universal or catholic; it is meaningful and transformative in any historical situation, including our own. Our work it is to bring the Church's symbolism to bear on the basic controlling human symbolisms of the present day.

What are the controlling symbols of our day? That is not easy to say, and social psychologists are far from agreement when they discuss this matter. Yet some of them we can mention here to point to the task that faces us. There is the symbol of the modern city: that focus of man's work and achievement, that hectic world of rush and competition which man strives to flee by life in the suburbs but which draws him magnetically to itself, that compilation of wealth and creature comforts and distractions that promises happiness. There is the symbol of the politically free society: that situation in which presumably men are able to pursue their human destiny in self-determination, in which men can deal with one another in dignity and open honesty, in which men can hopefully educate their children and plan for the future. There is the symbol of the machine: a paradoxical symbol that points both toward increased human freedom and increased human enslavement. There is the symbol of the beautiful woman: a symbol that is so ambiguous in our society, a symbol of promised love and happiness, yet often a symbol of deep human betrayal.

All of these symbols — and these are but a few instances — bear in them deep human hopes and longings, bear basic value judgments about life and the pursuit of human happiness. Some of these hopes and judgments are valid, many are inadequate or even false. Yet these symbols will not be banished from our midst; they cannot be destroyed; they can only be transformed. That

Church which is the city of God, which is the society of those who are free with the freedom of the children of God, whose face is that of the beloved spouse of Christ, must be seen by men for what she is. When so seen, the Church as the Sacrament of Christ himself will redeem the symbolisms of our day and the men who are so deeply influenced by them.

Fourth, the men of our world today are beginning to seek earnestly for a true unity of mankind; and we in the Church must lead them to this. However, this point leads directly into the second great goal of the Vatican Council of which I spoke at the beginning, work toward the reunion of Christians; so let us move on to a brief consideration of the role we must play in helping to achieve this goal.

History, particularly the history of the late medieval councils that worked for reunion, teaches us that it is not enough to work out Christian reunion on top authoritative levels; there must be a preparation for and acceptance of reunion on all levels if it is to be truly effective and lasting. So, while the work progresses at high levels — and let us hope that it continues to progress and come to final term — ours is the important task of readying ourselves and our friends, our children and our neighbors, for reunion. It is obvious that we must seize every opportunity to acquaint ourselves with the position which our separated brethren actually hold on important issues of revelation; correct factual information about our respective beliefs is one of the first steps we must make. However, I think that there are certain elements in the understanding of our own Catholic belief that will help us as we approach the questions of Christian reunion.

We must make the truth that the Church is truly Catholic become a living reality for us; we must rid ourselves of the tendency we have to think of the Church of Christ in Latin forms alone, to think of Christianity as an occidental reality. We are accustomed to the idea that the Church is universal in the sense that it is meant to be brought to all parts of the world where men need salvation; we must also become accustomed to the idea that the Church belongs properly to all parts of the world, that it is not Roman, nor American, nor European, but catholic. Some are beginning to talk in this way; we are definitely progressing in sympathy with other cultures and (in a strictly religious context) with other liturgies. But we must be careful that we do not view other liturgies and other forms of expressing Christian belief as mere variants from our Latin expression which, we assume, is the best.

Again, we must bring ourselves to realize that the Church is catholic in her approach to truth; there is no genuine intellectual achievement that is not meant to be used by her in understanding more clearly her revealed heritage. Contemporary man possesses many areas of valid insight into truth that as yet have not been incorporated into our theological understandings. By her nature the Church is meant to be open to all this truth, we must see to it that we reflect this universal openness in our persons.

One of the gravest problems we face as we undertake the task of reunion is the lack of common vocabulary, of common categories of religious thought. For four hundred years Catholic and Protestant thinking, philosophical and theological, have been growing steadily apart; for more than twice that long the thought breach has developed between Latin and Orthodox Christianity. Anyone who has been involved in some ecumenical discussion knows how frequently misunderstandings can arise because a word is understood differently by different religious traditions. Fortunately, there is a ground of meeting that has been provided us by Sacred Scripture; beginning from an objective study of the sacred text we can build a thought world and a vocabulary that is genuinely common.

This seems to have a rather important series of implications. It would seem that it is not enough to give ourselves over to the objective reading of the Bible; we must rather bring ourselves to the point at which we can think in biblical categories and words about all the major points of Christian revelation. This is not to deny the value of scholastic precisions and language; this provides valuable clarification and is an integral part of the Church's developing understanding of the Scriptures themselves.

We should make every effort to become familiar, so far as in us lies, with scholastic thought; but if we can think of Christian realities only in these terms, we will be incapable of communicating religious ideas to educated men of our day. On the other hand, if our understanding of the Christian message is profoundly biblical, we will automatically be conditioning ourselves for ecumenical discussion.

Another need that will face us as we move toward reunion is that of understanding the Church as an historically developing reality. If we are not conscious of the way in which the Church existed in former times, do not see that a fair amount of the externals of the Church as we now know her are somewhat accidental, it will be impossible for us to assess the historical problems connected with ecumenical discussion. On the other hand, if we come to view the Church as the vital reality she is, picture the Church over the centuries in the exercise of her role, honestly face the ups and downs of Christian life, then the sad events of the Greek Schism and the Reformation will become more understandable.

One of the most important steps toward reunion is the vitalization of sacramental life. A large part of Protestant and even Orthodox differences with the Catholic Church is connected with our practice of the sacraments. Yet there is a new awakening to the importance of sacrament among those outside the Catholic Church, just as there is a welcome awakening to sacrament within Catholic circles; and if our living of the sacraments becomes a genuine expression of a mature Christian faith, if our sacramental actions bespeak clearly the mystery of Christ working in our midst, then sacraments — above all the Eucharist — can effect that unity of men in Christ which they signify. Clearly the burden rests heavily on us to immerse ourselves, intellectually and with our whole person, in sacramental living so that our participation in these focal Christian acts is intelligent and genuine.

These, then, are a few areas of the task which is ours, the task of helping to attain the goals that the Church has set for herself in the council summoned by Pope John.

RABBI REUVEN SIEGEL

THE ECUMENICAL MOVEMENT AND THE JEWS

THE Jewish community, over the course of 1900 years, reacted to no Pope as did the Jewish community with warmth and feeling to Pope John XXIII.

Of all the Popes he struck the warmest note in terms of feeling among the Jewish community. He did so not only because he had, while Papal Legate in the Near East, during the years of the Nazi holocaust, made visas available for Jews to help save them from slavery and death, but also because he saw to it while Pope that concern for Jews be shown in the liturgy of the Good Friday service. He ordered the prayer, "Oremus et pro perfidis Judaeis" — "Let us pray for the perfidious Jews," which was part of the Good Friday service, to be removed from the liturgy of the Church. Indeed, the story as it was reported in the newspapers created an especial warmth as well. It was reported that the celebrant of Good Friday services in St. Peter's forgot the Pope's directive and included the words, "Oremus et pro perfidis Judaeis." But Pope John, on hearing the phrase, asked the celebrant to go back, to recite the prayer once more, this time omitting the offensive phrase. The story was later denied in official newspapers and statements; nevertheless a feeling of warmth, whether this incident occurred as it was reported or not, pervaded the Jewish community, which felt that here, within the life of this man, there was a heart, a feeling for humanity, a love stretched outward.

Pope John is said to have looked at the window and said that he was going to open it and allow fresh air into the Church. The Jewish community had the feeling that, when Pope John opened the window in the form of the Ecumenical Council, he was not only opening a window to allow fresh air into the Church but also opening a window to allow Catholics to look outside to see other races, other religions, and other groups, and to regard them with a measure of interest and feeling. The papal encyclicals which were issued by Pope John XXIII, *Mater et Magistra* and above all *Pacem in Terris*, gave encouragement and hope to all men by their stress on human solidarity and brotherhood. Indeed, in *Pacem in Terris*, Pope John declared that "Every human being has the right to freedom in searching for truth and in expressing and communicating his opinions. . . . Every human being has the right to honor God according to the dictates of an upright conscience."

Because of his actions and words, Pope John impressed everyone with the feeling that here was a man who was concerned about religious groupings outside the Church. Spontaneously men of all creeds turned with warmth toward him. When he took ill, prayers were recited in Synagogues for his recovery. And, when he died, Jews joined in the mourning.

When the Vatican Council was assembled, the interests of the various groups, not only of Catholics, but also of Protestants and other religious bodies throughout the world, was quite intense. Jews were interested in the Council because it showed, in striking fashion, that the Church *was* concerned about the problems of renewal and above all that the Church was not really a monolithic structure, that there were variations in points of view and the ability to argue, and to argue rather fiercely, as to what the direction and tendency of the Church should be. Jews were concerned whether or not there would be a statement about the Church's position on religious liberty; whether or not there would be a statement on the Church's position on the separation of Church and State; whether there would be a statement on religious pluralism and the rights of other religious groups.

One must admit that the Jews, as Protestants at times, have had what can be called a kind of mistrust and suspicion of the Constantinian reflex, that is, the traditional resort to the machinery of the State to advance the purposes of the Church. Consequently Jews are vitally interested in seeing how far the Council will progress in settling and, hopefully, dissipating such fears.

Of special interest to Jews is the matter of Catholic-Jewish relationships. These will be considered at greater length.

A number of statements issued with regard to the Vatican Council, and some assemblies relating to it, created a great measure of excitement and enthusiasm in the Jewish community. In January, 1962, for example, a fraternal agape was sponsored by the Pro Deo University in Rome at which Cardinal Bea spoke to eighteen non-Catholic religious groups. They included Protestants, Jews, Moslems, Hindus, Buddhists, and Copts. In the course of this particular meeting Cardinal Bea made a remarkable statement: "The greatest challenge to our generation is the problem of group antagonism and it is the primordial duty of all groups of mankind to unite for the purpose of overcoming hatreds of the past." Naturally declarations of this kind, made by responsible and thoughtful persons, aroused great expectations in all men. Moreover, when the Council was assembled, invitations were extended to all Christian groups to send observers. There is even a report that the Jewish community was also invited, unofficially, to send observers to the Council. This created a number of problems in the Jewish world. Jewish life has no hierarchy. We have no authoritative head who can decide what the policy should be and what the Jewish reaction should officially be to such an invitation. When an unofficial invitation was extended, inviting Jews to send observers from among Jewish secular organizations concerned about the fight with anti-Semitism, a difficult problem was raised. Some of these Jewish organizations, without, as I say, having received any official invitation, began to leak articles to newspapers and spread the story that they were ready and willing to send observers to the Council. One was the World Jewish Congress, whose president announced that an observer would be sent, an observer who, merely by virtue of his being named, at once created tremendous problems. For he held an official post in the State of Israel. Thus his presence as an observer had political implications. Religious organizations within Jewry, in particular the Orthodox, announced their opposition to sending formal observers to the Ecumenical Council. They felt that since the Council was to deal with doctrinal and organizational problems, and with questions relating to *Christian* unity, Jews would evidently not be involved in any formal way with the work of the Council. Conservative and reform groups joined the Orthodox in advocating a policy of opposition to any formal, official, participation as observers of the Council. Consequently, no formal Jewish observers could be sent to the Vatican Council. Yet one must not misunderstand this fact; it is necessary to understand that the absence of a formal observer in no way indicates that there is an absence of interest and a vital concern with what is going on at the Vatican Council itself. It is just that the Jewish position in respect to its relationship with the Church made it impossible for a formal observer to be sent to an Ecumenical Council. But the Jewish community itself has been reading the newspapers very thoroughly and our Jewish publications have covered in great detail aspects of the Council, particularly those that have dealt with relationships of the Church and the Jews.

After the Council was summoned, it was reported that Cardinal Bea had had instructions from Pope John himself that a paper was to be prepared and submitted to the Vatican Council dealing with the Jews and the relationship of the Jews and the Church. Cardinal Bea again had a problem. Many different Jewish organizations wanted to be spokesmen and to discuss the matters which might be included in the memorandum. Cardinal Bea met with Jules Isaac of France, an outstanding Jewish scholar there, and then visited the United States. Here Jewish organizations had finally agreed that Cardinal Bea should not be swamped with a superabundance of spokesmen. Rabbi Abraham Heschel of the Jewish Theological Seminary of America prepared a paper on the Jewish point of view and had a series of dialogues, which were reported to be very friendly, with Cardinal Bea, expressing the areas of Jewish concern and the subjects which the Jewish community felt should be included in any discussion of Jewish-Catholic relations. There have been no official reports, you can well understand, as to what was discussed between Cardinal Bea and Rabbi Heschel, or what the Jewish memoranda were which were submitted. But there is a good measure of conjecture which is bound to be reasonably accurate. It is reasonable to assume that the items which were submitted by the Jewish community covered the following areas: (1) the matter of Catholic-Jewish tensions and proposals for relieving them; (2) the matter of liturgical references in the Church which have in the past lent themselves to misinterpretation or to misuse; (3) the question of textbooks in use in schools and matters of the catechism. In brief, areas of instruction to the young which have sometimes led to intergroup difficulties.

A few years ago Yale University made a study of Protestant textbooks; St. Louis University, of Catholic textbooks; and Dropsie College, of Jewish religious school textbooks, in order to see how these texts discussed the beliefs of others and the attitudes they created with respect to persons of differing religious convictions. These were submitted to the respective groups and the St. Louis University report was said to have been submitted to Cardinal Bea. In 1962 Cardinal Bea prepared a memorandum on the Jews, intending it as the basis for discussion at the Council. For a while there was a measure of silence about Cardinal Bea's report. There was no official word on the time when the paper would be submitted or any action taken with regard to it. A number of points covered in the paper were leaked to the press. I say "leaked to the press" in a kindly sense. It was meant to be leaked to the press by Father Gregory Baum and Monsignor Oesterreicher. Then the late Father Gustave Weigel, who was then in Rome as a *peritus*, reported to the press that the paper on the Jews had been prepared but that it would not be presented at the Council. He expressed concern that the paper might be construed by the Arab States as a pro-Israel political gesture. After Father Weigel issued that statement, there was an immediate denial from the Vatican that the paper would not be presented. It was reported that the matter had been only temporarily tabled. This was in 1962, toward the end of the year. At the opportune moment the paper would be introduced at the Vatican Council, so the Vatican report ran. The problem was essentially one of time. And this is exactly what occurred. The paper was not released during 1962 but it was made public during the second session of the Council.

Why do I, a rabbi, believe that a paper from the Church about the Jews is important, indeed necessary, in our time? To be very candid about it — and this is not a matter of dredging up old hatred and old difficulties — Christian and Jewish relations have not been the very best in the past. This is even understating the case. There have been many enmities, many hatreds, much bitterness, much pain, much suffering. We know that Jewish-Christian relations during the early centuries of the Christian era were polemical, marked by conflict. Christianity was finding its identity and developing its forms and, as it were, detaching itself from its Jewish origins. The theme of the deicide, the murder of God-man, of Jesus the Christ, was stressed. The Jews, who had been God's Chosen People, who by right should have accepted Jesus as their Redeemer and Messiah, had become in the eyes of Christians an accursed race, a stubborn people who had rejected the One promised to the Patriarchs of old. The Wandering Jew bore the stigma of the mark of Cain upon his head, and generation after generations suffering was regarded as fitting and proper for Jews by virtue of the sin they had committed, the sin of deicide. And the bitterness born of those early years, of the polemics of the Jewish Synagogue and of the early Christian Church, sharpened and developed. After Christianity became the state religion of the European continent, many of these aspects of the hatred were put into the form of law.

Most of the ecumenical councils of the past, when they did treat of Jews, were anything but kind. These councils were concerned with destroying any influence Jews might have upon Christians. They were concerned with preventing the return to Judaism of baptized Jews and with devising means to convert Jews to Christianity. Hence both the ecumenical and local councils, particularly during medieval times, aroused in Jews a great measure of bitterness, of resentment, of hurt.

Thus, for example, there was a series of councils, beginning as early as the fourth century, which prevented any familiar relationships between Jew and non-Jew, even to the extent of forbidding Christians to eat together with Jews. The Third Lateran Council, held in 1179, forbade Christians to act as servants to Jews. Christians must not live together with Jews, nor in the same quarters. New synagogues could not be built; old ones could be repaired only when dilapidated but on no account beautified.

The Fourth Lateran Council went even further in reducing Jewish status in the continent of Europe. Canon 67 of the Fourth Lateran Council required Jews to pay a special Easter tax of six denarii. Jews were required to wear a special dress, a special badge, a special hat. They were not allowed to leave their homes during Easter. It is worth noting the fact that the Christian feast of Easter and the Jewish feast of the Passover coincide. As a result many Christians believed that the Jews dressed up at this time to rejoice over Christ's crucifixion. Such, of course, was not the reason for Jewish festivities at Passover time. But this misunderstanding helped create an atmosphere of distrust and hatred.

In 1434 the General Council in Basel — and its act was later renewed by the Synod of Milan in 1565 — compelled Jews to listen to sermons for their conversion.

Moreover, during the Middle Ages many charged the Jews with desecrating the Eucharistic host. The accusation was frequently made that Jews so hated Christ that they wanted to kill him again and again in his Eucharistic presence. Thus too arose the calumny that the Jew needed the blood of Christians for the baking of the matzo, his unleavened bread.

All of these were part of the climate of the Middle Ages, part of the concrete relationship between the Church and the Jews. It was a very bitter relationship, and the results of some of these councils were very, very unhappy for the Jewish community.

In our own time, we must understand — and this is a point I would make very clear — the Church is not responsible for anti-Semitism. There were anti-Semites before the Church. Back in pagan times there was prejudice against the Jews. There are many reasons for anti-Semitic feeling — reasons which may be social, psychological, economic, political. There may be any number of factors. But we must honestly be able to admit that the relationship between the Church and the Synagogue through all these years has never been a happy one. It was not based on tolerance and understanding. We must understand, too, that there were many bishops and many popes who went counter to these synods and provided protection for members of the Jewish community, but overall the relationship was not happy through all those years.

Indeed into modern times one of the problems has been to what measure this anti-Jewish feeling, this feeling that the Jew is a Christ-killer, has been a sop to the bigot who says that "after all the Jew is simply getting what he deserves after what he did to Christ during those years."

Barbara Ward Jackson, a Catholic, a writer in England, a very, very astute woman specializing in writings along a political line, wrote this as a sort of a challenge:

> As the memory of Auschwitz and the gas chambers fades, is there a chance that such horrors could recur? This is a question of particular and urgent . . . force in Europe, for whatever the reactions of antisemitism in other lands, in other cultures, only in Europe is the apocalyptic climax reached in which six million people were exterminated for being Jews. No one can be sure of the answer to this question unless another is asked. Have all the roots of the old anti-semitism been finally torn from Europe's conscious and unconscious mind?
>
> And this is a question of particular poignant force for Europe's Christians, since whatever other sources there may be of antisemitism one immensely strong tap root has been the historical antagonism between Church and Synagogue and the tragically perverted Christian interpretation of the Biblical role of the Jews.

Christian attitudes to Jews are all too often fixed in childhood by a reading of the Gospels in almost primitive terms of "goodies" and "baddies." The Jews reject Jesus. Caiphas simply hands him over to Roman power. Judas betrays him for money. The crowd howls that his blood will be upon them and on their children.

These simple images of treachery and violence invade the childish mind with the force of myth and unconsciously the Jew is seen as evil. This in turn influences attitudes of distrust and dislike. These then induce in the Jew a set of hostile or defensive reactions which confirm the original Christian dislike. All too often there is no later reexamination of early attitudes. Myth takes over. And antisemitism is confirmed. It need hardly be underlined how fantastically far removed is this myth from Christianity's true doctrine. At the universal level, to believe in the possibility of collective guilt, handed on generation after generation to innocent people wholly removed from the original tragedy is to make nonsense of two fundamental Christian concepts, the redeeming compassion of God and the personal moral responsibility of His creatures.

Cardinal Bea also dealt with this particular problem. Why should the Church, after all these years, prepare a paper for submission to the Vatican Council about the Jews? In replying to this question, the Cardinal said:

It was because of the violent and criminal outburst of anti-Semitism in Nazi Germany thirty years ago. That outburst was accompanied by a far-reaching campaign of propaganda against the Jews, based to some extent on the deliberate misuse of Scripture. Accordingly [he continued] it was quite possible that Nazi purposes had had an influence on some Christians that had not been entirely removed. National Socialism or Nazism in no sense sprang from the Church, but sought to use the teachings of the Church to condemn the Jews. The text before the Council is among other things an effort to clear away once and for all any vestiges of such misuse of Catholic teaching in the lives of Roman Catholics.

Cardinal Bea went on to explain that this document was significant. He acknowledged that Roman Catholic teaching, in dealing with the death of Christ, had been influenced by such lines as "His blood be upon us and upon our children" from Matthew, Chapter 27. He also acknowledged that Jesus had spoken severely to the Pharisees (cf. Lk 9:42–46). But the Cardinal reminded his hearers that while Jesus was dying on the Cross, He said, "Forgive them, Father, for they know not what they do." Cardinal Bea also cited St. Paul's Epistle to the Romans (11:1), which asks "Has God cast away his people?" And he replied, "God forbid!"

This, then, is the basis for the paper on the Jews which was submitted by Cardinal Bea to the Council. There are five major points with which the paper deals. Summarized, they are as follows:

1. The Church has a deep bond with the Chosen People of the Old Testament.

2. The responsibility for the death of Jesus falls on all mankind. This was established at the Council of Trent, but, unfortunately, it did not filter down to the local level of teaching and catechetical instruction. It is unjust to call the Jewish people deicides or to consider the Jews cursed by God.

3. The Church can never forget that Christ's Mother and the Apostles were born of Abraham's stock.

4. The death of Jesus Christ cannot give rise to disdain or hatred or persecution of the Jews.

5. Catholic priests and all Catholics are admonished never to teach a contrary position and, furthermore, are urged to promote understanding and esteem toward Jews.

When the paper was released, there was a great measure of favorable opinion toward it in the Church, particularly in European countries and on the part of American bishops and cardinals. There was also some measure of opposition. Some of this opposition was understandable from the Jewish point of view because some of the primates of Eastern Churches in Arab countries felt that there might be a confusion that this document took sides, as it were, in the matter of the Arab-Israel dispute. Cardinal Bea very firmly and very clearly noted that the document did not apply to these political problems of the Arab States and Israel;

this was a religious paper dealing with the causes of past animosities and hatreds and was meant to effectuate a change in the relationship of Church and Synagogue. Some cardinals and bishops said that ecumenism refers to unity among Christians, and consequently Jews shouldn't be discussed at all. Some felt that the paper should not be discussed in the early schema on Christian unity but should be taken up later. Probably the most bitter opponent was Ernesto Cardinal Ruffini of Palermo, Italy:

> If the Jews were to receive honorable mention in the schema, then the text should treat those other religions whose members are often less hostile to the Church than the Jews and more open to conversion than the Protestants.

What was the reaction of the Jewish community to this paper? Understandably Jews welcomed it as a document long since overdue. There was not a single critical reaction for the paper. These five points can do much to develop understanding and proper feeling toward each group — whether Conservative, Orthodox, or Reformed — whichever the country of the world. The Jewish reaction toward this paper was favorable and very hopeful. Jews hoped that this would not simply remain a document for discussion but that it would have the vote of approval of the Church Fathers.

We live — all of us, Catholic, Protestant, Muslim, Jew, or whatever else we may be — in a time when we can be truly grateful to God that the time has come when a window has been opened. I am certain, as a rabbi, that it is extremely significant and manifests the vitality of the Church when we see it able to discuss itself, update itself, act on the use of the vernacular in the sacraments and the like. But, as a Jew, I look upon this Council as not only an opening to allow fresh air *into* the Church, but also as an opening for Catholics to look outside and see other groups and understand that the crying problem of our time is the overcoming of group antagonisms. All religious people today, whether Catholic, Protestant, Jew, Buddhist, Copt — whatever their religion may be — face the problem of religion versus antireligion. Not simply irreligion but antireligion. There are many areas in which men of goodwill can work together with respect and understanding for one another. This Ecumenical Council also implies the coming of a time when we shall be able to talk to one another, to learn to understand one another and to respect one another, and, through the process of speaking to one another, to become firmer in our own convictions and more dedicated to our own purposes but equally respectful of the rights and the view of our neighbor.

Dr. Abraham Heschel, who participated in dialogue with Cardinal Bea, spoke on the Catholic Hour on May 26, 1963. He spoke on the *Church and the Council — a Non-Catholic View.* I would like to conclude with some of his remarks as to what the problem of our time is and what he, as a non-Catholic, feels can be accomplished by the Vatican Council:

It is customary [Dr. Heschel says] to blame secular science and antireligious philosophy for the eclipse of religion in modern society. It would be more honest to blame religion for its own defeats. Religion declined, not because it was refuted, but because it became irrelevant, dull, oppressive, and insipid. When faith is completely replaced by Creed, worship by discipline, love by habit, when the crisis of today is ignored because of the splendor of the past, when faith becomes an heirloom rather than a living fountain, when religion speaks only in the name of authority rather than with the voice of compassion, its message becomes meaningless. The great spiritual renewal within the Roman Catholic Church, inspired by Pope John XXIII, is a manifestation of the dimension of depth of religious existence. It already has opened many hearts and unlocked many precious insights. There is a longing for peace in the hearts of man but peace is not the same as the absence of war. Peace among men depends upon a relationship of reverence for each other. Reverence for man means reverence for man's freedom. God has a stake in the life of man — of every man. It was in the spirit of that theology that Cardinal Bea announced his intention to prepare a constitution on human freedom for presentation at the next session of the Council in which the Fathers would be asked to come out emphatically with a public recognition of the inviolability of the human conscience as the final right of every man no matter what his religious beliefs or ideological allegiance. Cardinal Bea has stated further that the axiom, "Error has no right to exist," which is used so glibly by certain Catholic apologists, is sheer nonsense, for error is an abstract concept incapable of either rights or obligations. It is persons who have rights and, even when they are in error, their right to freedom of conscience is absolute. In the words of Pope John's encyclical, *Pacem in Terris,* "every human being has the right to freedom in searching for truth and in expressing and communicating his opinion. Every human being has the right to honor God according to the dictates of an upright conscience." Man's most precious thought is God, but God's most precious thought is man. A religious man is a person who holds God and man in one thought at one time, at all times who suffers in himself harms done to others, whose greatest passion is compassion, whose greatest strength is love and defiance of deep despair.

This was the contribution of Pope John XXIII and is expressed in the Vatican Council. Particularly as Jews we feel this with regard to the paper prepared by Cardinal Bea about the Jews. We hope and pray that this will be translated into the doctrine of the Church, that it will be voted upon, it will be acted upon, that it will become part of the catechism and part of the instruction taught by teachers in local parishes and that this age-old lie, the era of horrible relationships between Church and Synagogue, will be rectified in our time, that group antagonism will disappear, and that a dialogue, a brotherly dialogue, will be the contribution of the Council to our generation and to future generations.

A PROTESTANT THEOLOGIAN LOOKS AT ECUMENISM

AN AMERICAN Protestant of my generation is likely to consider himself quite at home with ecumenism. In the decade before the Second World War the World Council of Churches was struggling to birth and, for many of us who were then young, the ecumenical movement was the most exciting development on the Christian scene. The atmosphere of the Roman Catholic Church today is often reminiscent of those years.

From one point of view, to be sure, our initiation was an easy one. Most of the interest related to the consolidation of Protestant bodies which had little religious or theological justification for separate existence. There was only too much to do along this line, and there still is. Scores of mergers have been effected, to be sure, and the pace seems to be quickening. But the difficulties were often more administrative than theological, as, e.g., in the case of the United Church of Canada.

This is not to say that Protestant understanding of ecumenicity has been merely pan-Protestantism. Some indeed have been interested only in that, but more than forty years ago in the early days of the movement objections were raised to using the word "ecumenical" unless Rome were also in prospect. It would seem a parody to designate as "ecumenical" a pan-Protestant body, consolidated perhaps in part on anti-Romanism. The developing Protestant and Orthodox ecumenical structure has carefully kept open the door to Rome. And within the movement the Anglo-Catholic and Orthodox spokesmen have constantly reminded those Protestants who needed it of the half of the Christian world in the Roman obedience who were still outside the conversation.

It has often seemed, in fact, that there is hardly a major issue between Roman Catholicism and Protestantism, apart from the questions connected specifically with the papacy, which has not been under debate in the World Council for years. Justification by grace and by works, Scripture and tradition, the eucharistic sacrifice, veneration of saints and the Virgin, various theories of apostolic succession, episcopal and otherwise, and their connection with the "validity" of sacraments — on all of these a generically "Catholic" view has been vigorously maintained in World Council gatherings. A Protestant observer at the Vatican Council is not likely to feel that he has been injected into a totally new realm of discourse.

Nevertheless we now have a new situation. The transformation in the relations of Roman Catholics to other Christians which has been effected by the Vatican Council is astounding, in Cardinal Bea's phrase, "a true miracle." Who would have believed it possible five years ago, or three? There is no doubt that the initiative and leadership of Pope John has been far and away the most important factor in the revolution of recent months.

Protestants, it seems to me, should accept the revolution with gratitude and acknowledge with admiration and joy the religious vitality disclosed in it at so many points. They will need to do some careful rethinking. They should be careful not to be too sure beforehand of what may or may not be possible, since God may be in this thing.

On the other hand, we must sooner or later get down to cases. There has been an understandable caution on both sides against reviving ancient animosities. The change in tone and attitude and the new personal contacts are still too new to bear much strain. But a consolidation of the gains will require a definition of continuing disagreements, as well as a clearing away of misunderstandings and prejudice. We must be prepared for new insights which may strengthen the bonds of community, and for the identification of deep differences. This is in part what we mean by ecumenism, and the task of dialogue.

Not all people mean the same by ecumenism and dialogue. No doubt most Roman Catholic visitors in Protestant discussions are somewhat uncertain as to the status they are supposed to hold. There was a similar ambiguity for Protestant observers at the Vatican Council. It is no criticism of our treatment as guests at the Council — an unfailingly courteous and generous reception — to say that we were aware that a significant section of the hierarchy felt that it had been a mistake to invite us and hoped that the invitation would not be repeated. What did "ecumenism" mean to such men? It was not a word they would have chosen, but since even the Protestant and Orthodox sense of the word had been given authoritative status, it was necessary to express even un-ecumenical views in ecumenical language. Ecumenism consequently was in effect defined as conversion of the erring. Here there really is no call for "dialogue," since communication is needed in one direction only. Charity to the separated brother consists in setting him straight as accurately and fully as possible. You will be able to find Protestants who will be "ecumenical" to you in the same fashion.

A larger group of the fathers in St. Peter's, perhaps even the largest, seemed to think of ecumenism as a tactic of conversion, no doubt, but as a more sophisticated one, taking account of the psychological barriers. It came then to something like what the Orthodox and Anglo-Catholics call "economy," a degree of flexibility with the canons and of management of the truth, so as to set the more appealing aspects foremost and reserve the more distasteful for a more opportune moment. This is a diplomatic, irenical approach, avoiding controversy and polemics, seeking to win by kindness and suavity, similar to what in the mercantile world is called the "soft sell." No doubt some bishops hoped that there might be one or two conversions among the observers themselves — how could they have been better treated? You will be able to find Protestants to offer you such "ecumenical" treatment, even if less splendidly equipped.

A quite different conception of ecumenism was to be found especially among the bishops and theologians associated with the

Secretariate for Promoting Christian Unity. Here a dialogue with Christians other than Roman Catholics was urged, not just as a tactic of conversion, but first of all for the sake of the Roman Catholics involved. In many cases, it was pointed out, Roman Catholics — individuals, parishes, whole regions — had become one-sided and defective in their appropriation of Catholic truth. In the course of generations of debate with Protestants, for example, they might have come to neglect such matters as Bible study, the preaching of the Word, congregational participation in worship and the sacraments, simply because Protestants emphasized these things. Other matters, again, might have been stressed out of due proportion, just because they were known to disturb Protestants. Insofar as this had happened, a Roman Catholic who really listened to Protestant criticism might discover that he had neglected some of the riches of Catholic truth and might emerge a better Roman Catholic. Dialogue with separated brethren might thus become an instrument in the renewal of the Roman Catholic Church. Similarly a Protestant might learn more of the fullness of the Gospel as he freed himself from the distortions of anti-popery.

This understanding of ecumenism is very close to the views current in World Council circles as to the meaning of the dialogue there. There, too, members of church bodies which do not fully recognize each other nevertheless find it religiously useful to share their understandings of the faith. A famous declaration of the World Council Central Committee once made it explicit that "membership in the World Council does not necessarily mean that a member church recognizes all the other member bodies in the full and true sense." And it is notorious that some of the members do not in fact concede the full character of church to other members. They may and do believe that their doctrine is right and others are wrong, that they are of the true church and others are not in the full sense. But they also acknowledge that there is *something* of "church," some "elements" or "vestiges" of the true Church, even in these defective bodies. And if even in this minimal sense the true Church is somehow diffused and separated from itself, there is an obligation on Christians to seek to clarify and manifest its true unity. This is the purpose of dialogue.

What does it mean to say that there is something of "Church" in a Christian society? Surely it means that the separated brother holds to some aspects of Catholic truth, participates in some gifts of the Holy Spirit, which are mediated to him *by his Church*. There is no ecumenical dialogue unless both parties are within the faith and within the Church, not necessarily equally or in the same way, but in some way. An ecumenical dialogue is about the same Lord, the same faith, the one Church, the same God and Father in some fundamental sense.

It is not clear how far the Council acknowledges this contention. Protestant and Orthodox observers have some mixed feelings about the proposal to add representatives of other religions to the company of observers. There is no objection whatever, of course, to Roman Catholic conversations with Hindus, Buddhists, Moslems. But do the fathers think that they will have the same kind of conversation on the basis of an abstract monotheism, or a recognition of the divine in general, as with those who live out of the definitive disclosure of God in Jesus the Christ? For some all seem to be alike discussions between "Catholics" and "non-Catholics." But to Protestants there is an enormous difference as to whether or not the dialogue takes place within the faith and, in some sense, within the Church.

There are two ways (at least) of approaching the nature of the Church. At this moment in Rome the fathers are considering the Church in its aspect of "mystery," sacramentally, as the sum of the means by which God effects his redeeming will in Christ, and as the society of those brought into communion thereby, his "people" or "family." So considered, the center of the Church is readily identifiable, but it is difficult to know just where the outer limits are and where Christ is *not* present in the Spirit. A juridical or canonical definition, on the other hand, makes all this very clear. There are definite criteria of membership, and if you are not in, you are out. In this case it is the religious substance of the Church which evades containment in the juridical categories. The means of grace have in recent centuries escaped over the canonical walls and are used by the Holy Spirit, as it were, without canonical license. As the Lambeth bishops declared in 1920, "We thankfully acknowledge that these ['non-episcopal'] ministries have been manifestly blessed and owned by the Holy Spirit as effective means of grace." Baptism in the triune Name, Scripture, the creed, preaching and teaching the Word, prayer through Christ, eucharistic communion — all these and other means of grace are available to and used by as many Christians outside the Roman communion as within it. Most of the gifts, if not all, which Christ has bestowed on the Roman Church, He grants to those faithful not in communion with Rome. And by them these Christians are bound to Him and to each other and to the faithful in the Roman obedience in a concrete historical and trans-historical society.

We may suspect that the fathers are now wrestling with the question as to how the Church as mystery is related to the juridical institution. The Reformers agonized over this question in the sixteenth century and eventually came to the conclusion that the former was the deeper and essential reality, a reality to which the canonical, hierarchical, and administrative structure is an instrument. That is why they could take the stand they did as Catholic Christians, standing within the one Church and calling for the reform of its administration by the light of the gospel. There was never the slightest intention of leaving the Church; to start a new Church was inconceivable. How could there be more than one Church? When Luther heard that men were calling themselves "Lutherans" he protested "I have never been crucified for anyone!" He was simply doing what the pope and bishops should have done long since.

When Cardinal Sadoleto accused Calvin of forsaking the Church, Calvin replied with an analogy. Conceive an army in battle, he said, in which the officers had failed and deserted, and one without a commission, "seeing the soldiers routed and scattered and abandoning the ranks, raises the leader's standard and recalls them to their posts." Should he then be court-martialed for usurping the prerogatives of command? A Roman Catholic imagination may refuse to entertain the possibility of such opposition of the juridical hierarchy to the Church as mystery, but may admit the distinction of the two and the primary importance of the second. Surely it is in exploring the nature of the second that we have hopes of greater ecumenical understanding. Insofar as we stand on the juridical nature of the Church our possibilities are effectively reduced to the choice of cold war or hot. None of our canonical theories are adequate to the religious reality of the Church today.

Let me conclude with three observations on the dimensions of our ecumenical task.

First we may need to be reminded periodically of the futility of merely verbal resolutions of doctrinal divergencies. Skillful theologians may sometimes hit upon formulations which seem to satisfy everyone. Something of the sort seemed to happen with regard to the Reformation debate over justification by grace four hundred years ago at Regensburg, and then again at the Edinburgh Faith and Order Conference of 1937. But little came of it. Whatever the theologians said, the laymen felt "these people are not like us." There were still two societies in confrontation, with deep differences in worship and devotion, in ethics and discipline, in constitution and orders. Our differences color much of our living and must be reconciled by understanding and growing together at all levels and in all dimensions. The unity of the Church is not an administrative matter to be achieved by experts over the heads of the people. More than once before negotiators have thought they had achieved an institutional reconciliation of Roman Catholicism and Eastern Orthodoxy, only to have the settlement repudiated by the body of Church members. A unity based on mutual recognition, understanding, trust, and brotherhood is an achievement of long years and of thousands of dedicated laborers.

There is also a sense in which the task grows ever more difficult. We have all been made more vividly aware of the worldwide outreach of Christianity, what Archbishop Temple used to call "the great new fact of our time." It is only in recent times that Christianity has become in actual fact as well as aspiration a world religion. In this respect the contrast between the constituency of Vatican Council I and Vatican II is very striking. There are parallels also in the World Council of Churches. And this is ground for rejoicing. But it also means that every major political, social, racial, cultural antagonism in this explosive world is now rooted *within* the Christian community. It is the very success of the Christian mission which brings it about that Christ's disciples are now separated by a Bamboo Curtain as well as an Iron Curtain. Politics has been one of the greatest obstacles to ecumenical achievement from the beginning. Now we seem to be approaching a situation where the reconciliation and unity of Christians is inseparable from that of humanity. On the one hand the success of the mission seems to hang on the achievement of Christian unity, and on the other hand such success as is achieved makes the task of unity ever more formidable.

My third observation is that this ecumenical task has an eschatological character. It is a task to be pursued in history, but whose full resolution is transhistorical. Some of my Roman Catholic friends protest that this is to deprive it of seriousness and urgency. I trust this is not the case. It need not cut the nerve of our struggle with sin to assume that perfect holiness is not attainable in this life. We know Christ's will for the visible unity of His followers, as for their holiness. Is it not enough for us to do faithfully the work laid before us in our time, trusting to Him to bring all things to fulfillment in His time?

REV. JOHN MEYENDORFF

CONTEMPORARY ORTHODOX CONCEPT OF THE CHURCH*

THE schism between the Churches of Rome and Byzantium, which occurred in the early Middle Ages, is undoubtedly one of the most tragic events of ecclesiastical history. On the one hand, after the eleventh century, the Eastern Church identified itself more completely with the political and social system of the Byzantine Empire. This does not mean, of course, as it is often thought, that a cesaropapistic regime was established in the East, but this means that Eastern Christians practically ceased to imagine the Church outside the framework of a definite social structure, and later submitted themselves to various forms of ecclesiastical regionalism and nationalism. On the other hand, in the West, a tremendous doctrinal and institutional development took place after the schism, without being counterbalanced by the Eastern tradition. An Orthodox historian will see in this unbalanced and one-sided development the origin of the various crises which the Western Church had to face, and more particularly the big crisis of the Reformation. He believes that the protest of the Reformers against various doctrines and institutions of the Roman Church of the sixteenth century could have been avoided if the original and truly catholic ecclesiology of the early Church had been preserved in the West.

The schism of the eleventh century is now far away in the past. There is no doubt that political, social, and cultural elements

---

* Reprinted with permission from the 1961 *Proceedings* of the Society of Catholic College Teachers of Sacred Doctrine. The text was revised and enlarged by the author.

did play an important role in bringing it about, together with purely doctrinal issues. The political and cultural situation has nowadays changed radically. Opposition and estrangement between what were once East and West is gradually losing more and more ground. The Roman Church is indeed a universal organism and the Orthodox Church is actively present in the world which we are accustomed to call "Western." This is particularly true of the United States where we are bound to live together, sharing the same language, the same political system, and the same culture. The time is approaching when the historical and cultural differences which once opposed our two Churches will definitely join the realm of mere archeology. What will remain then are the *issues of faith,* which were already real during the Middle Ages and which we have to face now before any serious attempts at reunion.

Let us now turn from history to theology and try to suggest the main points of orthodox ecclesiology today.

The Church Catholic

When we confess in our Creed that the Church is "one, holy, catholic, and apostolic," we really mean that the Church to which we belong is not a human institution or organization, but that it is the *Church of Christ*. Christ is the *one* Lord and He is the holy One. He saves all men of all nations and all generations, and we know Him through the apostolic witness. "I am with you until the end of the world" (Mt 28:20). The presence of Christ is realized in the Church and through the Church, which is His Body, by the power of the Holy Spirit. The image of the Body, as used by St. Paul, had undoubtedly a eucharistic sacramental context: the Church is truly the Body of Christ when it celebrates the Supper, established by the Master for the commemoration of His death and resurrection, "until he comes" (1 Cor 11:26). In the sacrament of the Eucharist, Christ and the Church are truly one Body. This sacramental reality is the mode of presence which Jesus Himself has chosen and established. It is there, at the

Eucharist, that the Word of God is read and interpreted; it is around it that all the other sacramental acts are performed, it is there that the Church is truly the one, holy, catholic Church of Christ, "built upon the foundation of the apostles and the prophets, Jesus Christ himself being the chief cornerstone" (Eph 2:20).

From this Eucharistic conception of the Church, it follows that every community gathered together in the name of Christ is the *one Church catholic*. St. Ignatius of Antioch, writing around A.D. 100 to the Church of Smyrna, declares quite clearly: "Wherever Christ Jesus is, there is the catholic Church" (Smyrn. 8, 2).

The meaning of this word "catholic," which was applied to the Church for the first time by St. Ignatius, and which was to have a surprising fortune in Christian theological vocabulary, provides one of the major keys to the understanding of early ecclesiology. In the West, it was generally understood as "universal." However, if this was the meaning of the word, it is not quite clear, for example, why the early Latin translators of the creeds kept in the text the Greek form *catholica ecclesia* instead of using *universalis*. As a matter of fact, practically all the versions of the Creed, with the notable exception of the Slavic version (the Slavic word *sobornaia* used here does not mean "universal"), kept the Greek original. The reason for this phenomenon is that the various translators were aware of the difficulty of translating *katholikē* by a single word in any language. If *katholikos* is ever to be translated by "universal," it still does not have a geographical, but an ontological, connotation. As applied to the Church, "catholic" first of all implies the idea of *fullness:* etymologically, it derives from the Greek adverb *kathólou*, "on the whole," as opposed to *katā mēros*, "partially." What St. Ignatius meant when he spoke of the "catholic" Church is that wherever Christ is, there is the fullness of His indivisible Body. This is the reason why "catholic" was later used to describe the *true* Church as opposed to the schismatical or heretical groups, who refuse the fullness of the apostolic doctrine and the integrity of the life in Christ. The "catholicity" of the Church is a doctrinal, cosmic, and moral universality, and not merely a geographical one.

These remarks are important for our understanding of the nature of a *local* church, gathered around its bishop for the celebration of the Eucharist: this assembly *is* the Catholic Church, it *is* the fullness of the Body, because Christ, the Head of the Church is present among His disciples and "wherever Christ Jesus is, there is the catholic Church." A local church is not a *part* of the Body, it is the Body itself, which is symbolized most realistically in the Byzantine rite of the preparation of the elements, when the priest places on the paten parcels of bread commemorating Christ Himself, His Mother, all the saints, all the departed and all the living: in this Bread the whole Church is really present together with the Head. The catholicity of the Church undoubtedly includes the idea of a geographical universality of the Christian message, but the two notions are not coextensive; for we cannot identify the Body of Christ with the universal Church of 1964, since this would mean to exclude from it all the saints, all the departed, and to restrict it to the size of a visible organization.

However, the Body of Christ is sacramentally fully present in every local church, the universal unity of all churches remains an essential element of catholicity. How is it manifested and preserved? First of all in the unity of faith and sacramental life. Since the early days of Church history a confession of the right faith was required from a newly elected bishop, and this confession was to be accepted by the bishops of the neighboring churches gathered for his consecration. Letters of communion were to be exchanged between bishops of the major sees: these letters expressed the *identity* of all local churches in their common allegiance to the apostolic faith. The notion of "identity" of all churches in faith and life is therefore an important element of orthodox ecclesiology: the churches cannot essentially *complement* each other, because each one possesses the fullness of Christ's sacramental presence, but they can and they must recognize in each other the *same* faith, the *same* fullness, and the *same* divine life. Schism occurs when this recognition becomes impossible, when the orthodox churches cease to perceive the same divine integrity in other Christian communities. The early Church had known interminable doctrinal discussions on the divinity of the Son, on the two natures of Christ, on His two wills. The final solution, and the salvation of orthodoxy, always came through an effort of mutual understanding, of mutual support and of mutual recognition by the churches. The decisive role in the final triumph of Orthodoxy might have been played by Alexandria, by Caesarea, by Constantinople or by Rome, but unity in the true faith was always sealed by the *councils*, which were considered and still are considered by the Orthodox Church as the normal organs expressing the unity of all churches in the apostolic truth. The highest doctrinal authority for orthodox Christians is the council, and not the voice of a particular local church, because the council expresses a *consensus* of churches in all of which Christ dwells and which are all guided by the Holy Spirit.

However, even councils have erred and entered into history only as "pseudo-councils." This shows that finally Christ alone remains the Head of His Church, as is unanimously emphasized by all orthodox doctrinal statements, and that His presence in the Church is a miracle of divine faithfulness toward God's people.

The Church Apostolic

The Christian faith is first of all a faith in the historic facts of the death and resurrection of Jesus Christ, and these facts are known to us through the witnesses chosen by Christ Himself: "You are witnesses of these things" (Lk 24:48; cf. Acts 1:22, etc.). And the Apostles always felt this witness as being their primary responsibility, the very foundation of their ministry: "That which was from the beginning, which we have heard, which we have seen with our eyes, which we have looked on and touched with our hands . . . we proclaim to you, so that you may have fellowship with us" (1 Jn 1:1–3).

The ministry of the Apostles is therefore absolutely unique, because it is only through them that we know of the historical Jesus: through their writings, which constitute that which we call the book of the New Testament, and through their oral teachings preserved by the Tradition of the Church. The Church has no other foundation than that which was laid by the Apostles, because there is no other and there can be no other revelation than that of the historical Jesus Christ, "in whom are hid all the treasures of wisdom and knowledge" (Col 2:3). In order to be really Christ's Church, the Church must be apostolic.

By its very nature, however, the Church is a new form of divine presence among men: the sacramental form, established by Christ Himself. What the Apostles did before leaving this world was to establish, wherever they preached, communities of Christians united by the bond of the Eucharistic meal. Except in the very beginning, in the Judaeo-Christian community of Jerusalem presided by Peter together with the other Twelve (Acts 1–9), the Apostles did not normally perform sacramental functions in the local churches. St. Paul writes to the Corinthians that "Christ did not send him to baptize, but to preach the Gospel" (1 Cor 1:17). The very nature of the Church required another type of ministry, in accordance with the sacramental nature of the Church. And we learn from the Acts and the Epistles that the Apostles appointed "presbyters" or "bishops" for every community.

At the end of the first century, what we now call the "monarchical" episcopate was an accepted institution of the whole Church. Since every Christian community was established upon the Eucharistic celebration, someone had to take the place of the Master at the Table; since every community was the whole Body, someone had to perform the ministry of the Head. And St. Ignatius of Antioch could write: "It is when you obey the bishop as if he were Jesus Christ that you are living not in a merely human fashion but in Jesus Christ's way. . . . It is essential, therefore, to act in no way without the bishop, just as you are doing. Rather submit even to the presbytery as to the Apostles of Jesus Christ . . ." (*Trallians*, 2). Sacramentally, the bishop performs the ministry of Christ Himself; he is the high priest and the teacher of his community; he is the Head and the community is the Body. The episcopal ministry is essentially distinct from the apostolic since it is by nature local and sacramental and therefore different from the universal witness of the Apostles to the historical Risen Lord. However, according to St. Irenaeus of Lyons, the apostolic message transmitted to the Church is kept by the bishops, who by their functions in the community, possess a "certain charisma of truth" (*Adv. Haereses*, IV ii, 2). After the death of the last Apostle, the episcopate, individually in every community, or collectively at Council meetings, is the bearer of the Christian truth. The bishop's doctrinal and magisterial responsibility is undoubtedly a sacramental gift of God, but it can be exercised only in his own community, which elected him and with which he is linked for life. His ministry is not a power that he exercises *over* the Church, but *in* the Church. His responsibility is to be the minister of the Church's apostolicity and orthodoxy. In some sense, one can say that the Apostles were above the Church, since they were personally selected and appointed by Christ to be His witnesses. The bishops, on the contrary, only perform a necessary function of the Body itself: they have no personal witness to bear, but only to receive and to proclaim the apostolic tradition which belongs to the whole Church.

It is at this point that we reach one of the major disagreements between East and West from the Middle Ages down to the present time. And there is no better introduction to the ecclesiological problems which opposed Byzantium and Rome than the recent book of a Catholic scholar, Fr. Francis Dvornik, on "The Idea of Apostolicity in Byzantium and the Legend of the Apostle Andrew."[1] Without pretending to be a theological treatise, this book provides the theologian with invaluable historical materials on early Christian ecclesiology. One of the main conclusions of the book is that the Christian East has never accepted the idea that "apostolicity" was the only (or the main) criterion of authority in the Church. By "apostolicity" we mean here the actual foundation of a particular local church by a particular Apostle. Many

---

[1] *Dumbarton Oaks Studies*, IV, Cambridge, Mass., 1958. See also J. Meyendorff, "La primauté romaine dans la tradition canonique jusqu'au concile de Chalcédoine," in *Istina*, 1957, p. 463 ff.

churches in the East could claim this kind of "apostolicity"; however, neither Jerusalem, nor Antioch, nor Ephesus actually pretended to primacy, but Alexandria, and later Constantinople, did so, both being located in the two biggest cities of the Eastern Empire. The exclusive claim of Rome, which gradually took shape in the West, could therefore be understood in Byzantium only as a result of the political importance of the old imperial capital. This was the interpretation given in 451 to the Roman primacy by the Fathers of Chalcedon (canon 28) in connection with the establishment of the patriarchate of Constantinople. In the moments when the intervention of the popes was considered necessary and useful, the Easterners, in letters addressed to the West, happened to mention the role of St. Peter, but these mentions belonged rather to the realm of diplomatic politeness and never implied a clear recognition of Rome as the only final criterion of Christian truth.

The question of St. Peter and that of his succession has been recently studied by several orthodox theologians.[2] It is, without any doubt, a crucial problem in our relations, but it cannot be treated extensively here. What is to be said, however, is that this question can be settled only in the context of a more general ecclesiological setting. We have tried to show that for the Orthodox Christian — and this was, we believe, the case for the primitive Christian too — every local eucharistic community is *the whole* Church of Christ. St. Ignatius saw in the bishop and in the presbytery an image of Christ and of all the Apostles. This is the Church founded on Peter (cf. Mt 16:18), i.e., every local church is, inasmuch as it keeps the faith, confessed by Peter on the road to Caesarea Philippi. And Peter in the entire Greek Christian literature, both before and after the schism, is considered as the prototype of *all* bishops who by their very function are the bearers of the true faith. And this, as a matter of fact, appears to be exactly the theory of the *cathedra Petri* as expressed in the third century by St. Cyprian of Carthage in his *De catholicae ecclesiae unitate:*

---

[2] J. Meyendorff, N. Afanassieff, A. Schmemann, N. Voulomzine, *The Primacy of Peter in the Orthodox Church* (London: The Faith Press, 1963).

there is only *one* episcopal see, that of Peter, and every bishop, in his own community, shares in the same identical episcopate derived from Peter.[3]

The bishops in their own churches, and the episcopate taken as a whole, are therefore responsible in the Church for the apostolic Tradition. The Orthodox Church, however, does not recognize any visible automatic criterion of truth which would require positive obedience. The episcopal function belongs to the Church and does not rule *over* the Church. Individual bishops and groups of bishops may fall into heresy, and this has happened many times in history, but the Church has remained in the Truth. The Holy Spirit abides in the whole body of the Church and restores the apostolic Tradition after every temporary human failure. This lack of criterion does not mean that we share with our Protestant brethren in the idea of individual interpretation of the Bible: nothing in the Church is individual, and everything is done in common; nothing is purely natural and human, but everything is sacramental. This is why doctrinal issues are settled in accordance with the common mind of the Church and are sealed by the sacramental magisterium of the bishops, who generally meet in councils to rule on important questions. Seven councils are accepted as having a final, ecumenical, binding importance, but other equally important points of faith were settled by lesser councils and are also universally accepted; and other Truths again, which were never contested, are held as self-evident by the Tradition of the Church, without any formal definition.

One of the major contrasts between Orthodox ecclesiology and practically all Western concepts of the Church is the lack in the Orthodox Church of a clearly defined, precise, and permanent criterion of Truth, beside God Himself, Christ and the Holy Spirit, abiding in the Church. In the West, the increasingly developed theory of papal infallibility was opposed, after the collapse of the conciliar movement, by the Protestant antiecclesiastical affirmation of *Sola Scriptura*. The entire ecclesiological problem since

---

[3] Cf. M. Bévenot's recent edition in *Ancient Christian Writers*, 25 (Westminster-London: 1957), pp. 6–7, 102–108.

the sixteenth century has turned around this opposition. In Orthodoxy, the Church itself, acting always as a Body, and normally through the apostolic ministry of the episcopate, is the criterion of Truth. I do not know any better expression of the manner in which the Truth abides in the Church than that which was given in the second century A.D. by St. Irenaeus of Lyons:

> The preaching of the Church is everywhere consistent, and continues in an even course and receives testimony from the prophets, the apostles, and all the disciples — as I have proved — through (those in) the beginning, the middle, and the end, and through the entire dispensation of God, and that well-grounded system which tends to man's salvation, namely our faith; which having been received from the Church, we do preserve, and which always, by the Spirit of God, renewing its youth, as if it were some precious deposit in an excellent vessel, causes the vessel itself containing it to renew its youth also. For this gift of God has been entrusted to the Church, as breath was to the first created man, for this purpose, that all the members receiving it may be vivified, and the communion with Christ has been distributed throughout it, that is the Holy Spirit, the earnest of incorruption, the means of confirming the faith, and the ladder of ascent to God. "For in the Church," it is said, "God hath set apostles, prophets, teachers" (1 Cor 12:28), and all the other means through which the Spirit works; of which all those are not partakers who do not join themselves to the Church, but defraud themselves of life through their perverse opinions and infamous behavior. For where the Church is, there is the Spirit of God; and where the Spirit of God is, there is the Church, and every kind of grace; but the Spirit is truth (*Adv. Haereses,* III, 24, 1).

The Church is a sacramental organism, to which the Spirit communicates the Truth, and there is no need for any other, external criterion. The continuity of the Church in history, from the apostolic times until now, is a miracle of this divine presence, a witness of the divine faithfulness to the Church.

It has been pointed out that when Orthodox theologians want to define the present highest doctrinal authority in the Church, they sometimes affirm that an infallible authority belongs to the

Ecumenical Council, and sometimes they claim that decisions of
Ecumenical Councils must be subject to further reception by a
general consensus of the Church. In fact, there is no real contradiction between these two statements, since both the Councils and
the consensus are instrumented by the same Spirit, and are not
therefore human juridical institutions of government. It is undoubtedly true that there cannot be a higher body in the Church
than the universal episcopate, assembled together, but we also
know that some very great episcopal assemblies have actually
met and produced very unorthodox statements, as did many
Councils during the Arian controversy, and also the Council of
Ephesus of 449. They were rejected by the Spirit of Truth, abiding in the whole Church. As St. Irenaeus wrote: "Where the
Spirit of God is, there is the Church." The dogmatic struggles
and doctrinal controversies of the early Church would simply have
been unthinkable if the infallible Church had possessed an automatic, visible organ of infallibility.

The whole attitude of the Orthodox Church toward the very
problem of doctrinal *definition* is involved in this aspect of orthodox ecclesiology. Living communion with the fullness of Truth is
the very essence of Church life, simply because Christ Himself *is*
this indivisible fullness, and in the Church, in the Scripture, in
the sacraments, in the preaching, we meet Him, and not a system
of doctrines. This communion with the fullness is accessible now,
just as it was in the time of the Apostles: it is always the *same*
fullness, based upon what the eyewitnesses of Christ's resurrection have told us. Nothing can be added to it and nothing can
be subtracted from it, and no new revelation can come from God,
who has already given us full access in His Son to His own divine
life and truth. The apostolic Truth, however, must be expressed
and preached before all nations, in all languages, in all situations.
This is the task of the Church. Christian Tradition, therefore,
does not merely repeat the words of the Apostles, it preaches
and announces the living Word of God. Each generation is therefore entitled to this living Word, and, most particularly, each
generation must receive from the Church a living guidance in

dealing with the various *false* teachings which may appear. This is the precise and the only need which exists for dogmatic definitions. It has been expressed and repeated by several Councils. At Chalcedon, in 451, for example, the Fathers proceeded with their famous Christological formulation only after having proclaimed that the "wise and salutary formula of divine grace (the Creed of Nicaea-Constantinople) *sufficed* for the perfect knowledge and confirmation of religion, for it teaches the perfect doctrine concerning Father, Son, and Holy Spirit"; the new definition is therefore necessary only because certain persons undertake to "make void the preaching of the truth through their individual heresies."

The basis of what we call "dogmatic development" is therefore the negative necessity to protect the Church against false teachings. And we believe that the Church provides this kind of permanent guidance to her faithful every time the need arises, either through formal Ecumenical Councils, or through local Councils whose decisions are subsequently accepted by all local churches, or even only through an implicit rejection of doctrines foreign to the apostolic teaching. Here again, the Church, being a living organism, may use the means which are the best or the only possible in every concrete situation. Thus the Ecumenical Councils of the first eight centuries have settled triadological and christological issues; since then, at various times, local Orthodox Councils have met and have dealt with questions such as the nature of grace (Constantinople, 1341, 1351), the attitude toward Western Christians (Constantinople, 1285; Jerusalem, 1672), liturgical questions (Moscow, 1666–1667), ecclesiastical order (Constantinople, 1872). Some of these decisions have been included in the liturgical books and, in practice, are just as binding for all Orthodox Christians as the decrees of the Ecumenical Councils.

It appears, therefore, that the Orthodox Church has a concept of dogmatic development rather similar to that of the Roman Church, with the exception of two points:

1) The manner in which this takes place,

2) The moment when a doctrine implicitly held by the Church must necessarily become explicit. An Orthodox theologian will hold that this event *must* occur at the very moment when the need is felt. He knows, for example, that Roman Catholic theologians refer to the concept of dogmatic development when they explain the progressive evolution and growth of the Roman primacy between the first centuries and 1870, but he does not understand how an ecclesiological doctrine of such importance could have remained in the implicit stage during the early theological controversies. At that time, it was apparently just as much needed as today for the good order and welfare of the Church. There is no doubt, therefore, that a further dialogue between Orthodox and Catholics on this vital problem of dogmatic development would be one of the most needed elements in our future irenical relations.

Conclusions

In the Roman Catholic and the Orthodox Churches, ecclesiology has practically the same status of importance, inasmuch as we all agree on one important aspect of the New Testament revelation: Christ has established on earth one *visible* community, which is just as visible as His own Body. Since this community belongs to Him, it cannot be divided; it is essentially and by nature *one*. Both our Churches however claim to be this one, indivisible Church of Christ.

This belief and conviction has led the Orthodox Church today to a responsible concern for the unity of all Christians. Christian unity is not only a unity among men; it is, first of all, a divino-human unity, a unity of men in God, in the communion of His presence, in the common share of his vivifying gifts. True unity will not be achieved outside of the divine Truth, outside the true Church. It is precisely *this* conviction that has led many Orthodox leaders and theologians to take part in the "Ecumenical Movement" originated among Protestants. This movement, really prophetic and revolutionary if we think of the state of fractioning in which the Protestant world found itself a century ago, has appeared to these Orthodox leaders as a search by Protestants for the true Church. Those who pretend to possess this truth could not have remained apart from such a movement.

The Ecumenical Movement went through two major stages of development. At the first stage, before the last world war, it remained essentially a movement of individuals, interested in questions of church unity. After the last war, the Movement took the shape of a "World Council of Churches." This means that the ecclesiastical bodies themselves participate in the work of the Council. The by-laws, however, were drafted in such a manner that Orthodox participation was formally made possible. No particular conception of the Church was implied by the membership, no ecclesiological relativism was required; on the contrary, the Declaration of Toronto (1950) formally specified that a member-church was not necessarily supposed to consider the other churches as "churches" in the full sense of the word. The Orthodox delegates have always had the possibility to proclaim their own conception of Church unity. In Evanston (1956) they abstained from voting on the "Faith and Order" report, and published a separate declaration which proclaimed:

> When we are considering the problem of Church unity we cannot envisage it in any other way than as a complete restoration of the total faith and the total episcopal structure of the Church which is basic to the sacramental life of the Church. We would not pass judgment upon those of the separated communions. However, it is our conviction that in those communions certain basic elements are lacking which contribute to the fulness of the Church. We believe that the return of these communions to the Faith of the ancient, united and indivisible Church of the Seven Ecumenical Councils, namely to the pure and unchanged and common heritage of the forefathers of all divided Christians, shall alone produce the desired reunion of all separated Christians. For only the unity and fellowship of Christians in a common Faith shall have as a necessary result their fellowship in the sacraments and their indissoluble unity in love, as members of one and the same Body of the one Church of Christ.

. . . It is suggested in the Report of the Section that the road which the Church must take in restoring unity is that of repentance. We recognize that there have been and there are imperfections and failures within the life and witness of Christian believers, but we reject the notion that the Church itself, being the Body of Christ and the depository of revealed truth and "the whole operation of the Holy Spirit" could be affected by human sin. Therefore, we cannot speak of the repentance of the Church which is intrinsically holy and un-erring. For "Christ loved the Church and gave Himself for it, that He might sanctify it and, cleansing it in the washing of water and the word, that He might present it to Himself as a glorious Church, not having spot or wrinkle or blemish or any such thing, but that it should be holy and without blemish" (*Eph.* 5, 26–27).

. . . In conclusion, we are bound to declare our profound conviction that the Holy Orthodox Church alone has pre-served full and intact "the faith once delivered unto the saints." It is not because of our human merit, but because it pleases God to preserve "His treasure in earthen vessels, that the excellency of the power may be of God" (*II Cor.* 4, 7).[4]

The members of the Orthodox delegation knew that their con-ception of the Church was quite foreign to the vast majority of the participants. The great difficulty of the present Orthodox participation in the World Council comes from the fact that Orthodox and Protestants do not always see in the Council itself the same reality. For many Protestants, the Council is already a prefiguration of the eschatological *Una Sancta;* for the Orthodox, it is essentially a place of meeting and of brotherly dialogue. The opposition of these two conceptions which was particularly and strongly felt at the last Faith and Order Conference (Montreal, 1963), does however lead to a fruitful Orthodox-Protestant dialogue on ecclesiology.

Since the pontificate of John XXIII, the Roman Catholic Church stepped actively into this dialogue. The late Pope John undoubtedly felt all the importance of the ecclesiological issues which are at

---

[4] Besides the official reports of the Assembly, this text has been published in the *St. Vladimir's Quarterly,* Vol. 3 (Fall, 1954-Winter, 1955), No. 1–2.

stake between Orthodoxy and Rome, and so he called the Council, at which the question of the episcopate, in its relation to the see of Rome, is the key issue.

The question that an Orthodox stresses today is whether the Council will somehow counterbalance the decision of 1870 in its definition of the episcopate. The present stress on "collegiality," which dominates the Council's thinking, would be a real step forward toward further mutual understanding between Rome and Orthodoxy, only if it presupposed something of the theology of the local church, as sacramental fullness. In the Orthodox perspective, a Bishop, head of the "Catholic Church" in a particular place, possesses the fullness of Apostolic tradition and authority, and, as such, is a member of the universal episcopal collegium. All the members of the collegium are equal in their episcopate, and the Primacy of one of them can be envisaged only as a function of coordination, not of power *over* the collegium.

The crucial issue at the Council seems therefore to be whether the definition on "collegiality" will simply recognize in the episcopate a consultative body around the Supreme Pontiff — such a concept of collegiality will make further dialogue even more difficult — or whether a certain *interdependence* of authority will be admitted between the Pope and the bishops. Only the latter alternative would bring us closer to union.

The real and great significance of the brotherly kiss recently exchanged in Jerusalem lies in the fact that the Roman Pontiff has accepted, at least symbolically, to act and to be seen publicly as the Bishop of the local Church of Rome, which, according to St. Ignatius of Antioch, "presides in love."

FRANCIS CANAVAN, S.J.

CHURCH, STATE, AND COUNCIL

THERE are certain difficulties in writing at this time about the position taken by the Second Vatican Council on Church-State relations. One is that the Council has said nothing on the subject. A text on religious liberty was submitted to the Council before its second session closed but the Fathers took no vote on it. As a result, it does not even have the status of a text accepted as the basis of discussion. We do not know, therefore, whether it will come before the Council in the next session in its present form. Nor can we be sure that the document will be acted on at all by the Council.

Obstacles such as these have never been known to daunt journalists and certainly they are not going to stop me. Candor obliges me to admit, however, that I speak with no special authority and with very little inside information. All I can do is to trace the lines along which Catholic thought on Church-State relations (more precisely, on religious liberty) has been moving. That done, I will conclude with an analysis of the chapter on religious liberty set before the Council in its last session and on which we may hope the Council will act before it concludes its work.

Before I begin, let me clear away one possible source of misconceptions and of misinterpretation of what I shall say. I refer to a parochialism which may lead us to assume, quite unconsciously, that our time and place constitute a standard by which to test the performance of the Catholic Church as she has existed through twenty centuries and now exists in all parts of the world.

George Bernard Shaw described this mentality as he found it in Great Britain in his day, in these words:

> The more ignorant men are, the more convinced are they that their little parish and their little chapel is an apex to which civilization and philosophy have painfully struggled up the pyramid of time from a desert of savagery. Savagery, they think, became barbarism; barbarism became ancient civilization; ancient civilization became Pauline Christianity; Pauline Christianity became Roman Catholicism; Roman Catholicism became the Dark Ages; and the Dark Ages were finally enlightened by the Protestant instincts of the English race. The whole process is summed up as Progress with a capital P. [Note to *Caesar and Cleopatra*.]

I have quoted Shaw because we are now, and for some time have been, witnessing a marked development of Catholic doctrine regarding religious liberty. It would be a mistake, in my opinion, if we were to look upon this development as evidence that the Church is now awakening to the fact that History achieved its supreme moment in 1790 with the adoption of the First Amendment to the Constitution of the United States. History has been going on for a long while and is likely to go on for some time longer. Meanwhile, there is no particular reason to assume that we in the United States represent a pinnacle from which mankind has nowhere to go but down.

Nonetheless, there has been an evolution in Catholic doctrine which at first glance appears like a complete about-face. In 1864, Pope Pius IX, in his encyclical, *Quanta Cura*, denounced the "erroneous opinion, than which none is more fatal to the Catholic Church and the salvation of souls, and which our predecessor of happy memory Gregory XVI called a madness, to wit, that freedom of conscience and worship is every man's proper right. . . ." Almost a century later, in 1963, Pope John XXIII, in his encyclical, *Pacem in Terris*, proclaimed: "Every human being has the right to honor God according to the dictates of an upright conscience, and the right to profess his religion privately and publicly." The contrast between these two papal statements is, to say the least, striking.

To understand how we have come from Pius IX (and from Pius VI, Pius VII and Gregory XVI before him) to John XXIII, we must examine what it was in the doctrine of religious liberty which they condemned. In the paragraph immediately preceding the passage from Pius IX quoted above, the Pope said:

> Today there are not lacking men who apply to civil society the impious and absurd principle of Naturalism, as they call it; they have the audacity to teach that the perfecting of government and civil progress necessitates that human society be ordered and governed without any more attention to religion than if it did not exist, or at least without any differentiation between the true religion and the false.

Pius IX and his predecessors objected most strongly to the philosophy in the name of which the modern liberties of religion, speech, and press were claimed. This philosophy, which had furnished the French Revolution with its intellectual motor force, was, first, a form of naturalism. That is, it denied the whole supernatural order of divine revelation and of grace and asserted that human reason was sufficient to the solution of all human problems and that human strength of will was sufficient to carry the solutions into effect. The revolutionary philosophy was also a radical individualism, which made each man's reason his supreme guide and his individual will the source of all authority in society. Since the modern liberties were proclaimed as conclusions derived from this philosophy, it is not surprising that the Church's first reaction to them was one of energetic rejection.

The Church also had practical reasons for refusing to accept freedom of religion, speech, and press as social norms. Society, under the old regime, was officially Christian. The truth of the Christian religion and, in Catholic countries, of Catholicism was officially acknowledged. Christian standards of morality were understood to inspire laws. Marriage and other human relations were regulated by canon rather than civil law. Society in principle, whatever its defects in practice, aimed at realizing Christian standards of virtue on the basis of revealed Christian truth. The new liberal regimes were a repudiation of the whole centuries-old attempt to build a Christian society in the world. Again, it is not surprising that the Church reacted against liberalism in terms of flat condemnation.

At times, indeed, as in the famous last proposition of Pius IX's Syllabus of Errors, Rome seems deliberately to have chosen the language best calculated to offend the nineteenth-century liberal mind. The eightieth and last proposition in the Syllabus of Errors appended to the encyclical *Quanta Cura* of 1864 reads as follows: "The Roman Pontiff can and should reconcile himself to and come to terms with progress, liberalism, and modern civilization." Many a gentleman, on reading those words in the London *Times*, must surely have blinked and read the news report over again to learn whether the Pope did not approve rather than condemn this proposition. Alas, there was no doubt: the Pope roundly condemned the notion that he should reconcile himself with progress, liberalism, and modern civilization. What he meant was that neither he nor any other Catholic could accept the naturalism and rationalism which were assumed to be the heart of modern civilization. One may ask, nevertheless, whether His Holiness could not have found some less offensive way of saying so.

At the very time, however, that the Church rejected liberalism on the level of theory, she showed that she was able to come to terms with it on the level of practice. In 1832, in the encyclical *Mirari Vos*, Gregory XVI qualified as "madness" the proposition that "every individual should be given and guaranteed freedom of conscience." Yet, even as this encyclical was being written, the Pope refused to heed the advice of persons who wanted him to repudiate the Belgian Constitution of 1831, which was based on the principle of separation of Church and State and guaranteed the freedom of worship which he condemned in *Mirari Vos*. Not only that, he named as Archbishop of Malines the Vicar-General Sterckx, who had come to Rome to defend the Belgian Constitution before the Holy See.

Numerous other instances could easily be cited to show that the Church was willing to accept freedom of worship in practice, while disapproving of it in principle. To explain this apparent discrepancy between theory and practice, the famous distinction between thesis and hypothesis was worked out. The distinction is said to have been first explicitly formulated by the Jesuits of *La Civiltà Cattolica* in 1863. The principle underlying it was finely expressed by Leo XIII in his encyclical *Immortale Dei* of 1885, in these words: "While the Church considers that it is not right to put the various forms of worship on the same footing as the true religion, it does not follow that she condemns heads of states who, with a view to achieving good or preventing evil, in practice allow these various creeds each to have its own place in the state." That is to say, the thesis or theoretical principle is that the state must recognize and prefer the true religion, which is that of the Catholic Church. But circumstances can make operative the hypothesis, according to which the state tolerates several religions and perhaps even places them on the same plane before the law.

Catholics who write on Church-State relations today are rapidly abandoning the language of thesis and hypothesis. It leaves Catholics open to the charge that they are obliged by their own doctrine to set up Catholicism as the established religion whenever that is possible and to tolerate religious liberty as at best a necessary concession to circumstances. Nevertheless, we find in the papal statements of the past century certain positions which the Church has not relinquished today and will not give up even in the future. Among them are the following: There is a divinely revealed truth about man and his relation to God, of which the Church is the infallible custodian. Men are not free to take or leave this truth as they choose; it is God's will that they accept His revealed truth and live by it. Society as well as individuals must guide its activities in the light of this truth. Since the same persons are members of the Church and citizens of the state, Church and State must act in harmony so that men may achieve both their temporal and eternal goals.

These positions are permanent. Nevertheless, as Dr. A. F. Carrillo de Albornoz remarks in the study, *Roman Catholicism and Religious Liberty*, which he wrote for the World Council of

Churches (Geneva, 1959), today "it would be an understatement to say that, for *one* book or article [by Catholic writers] in favour of the traditional doctrine [of thesis and hypothesis], *ten* have been published defending universal religious freedom as 'thesis'; and we should note that they have all been published with the 'nihil obstat' of the Roman Catholic authorities" (p. 8). The statement in John XXIII's encyclical, *Pacem in Terris*, "Every human being has the right to honor God according to the dictates of an upright conscience, and the right to profess his religion privately and publicly," is only one of the latest, though certainly the most authoritative expression of this remarkable change in the Church's position regarding religious liberty.

Catholic thinkers have led the way in this change of front by reflecting upon three principal themes: the rights of the individual conscience, the requirements of the common good in a pluralist society, and the nature and functions of the state. The rest of this paper will be devoted to explaining these themes.

Certain principles concerning the individual conscience have been solidly established for centuries in Catholic theology: the act of faith is free and requires a free assent of the human will; no one may be forced to accept the Catholic faith against his will; and the individual is obliged to follow what his conscience clearly and inescapably tells him is the will of God, even though in fact his conscience should be wrong.

On the basis of these well-established principles, a number of Catholic writers have argued that the state must recognize and guarantee the individual's right to worship God in the manner which his conscience dictates. In fact, there is no one in the Church who would question this right in its minimal terms. Catholic Spain recognizes it. In that country no one is forced to become a Catholic or is subject to legal sanctions for abandoning the Catholic faith. Non-Catholics may and do have their own houses of worship. But — and this is the burden of complaints against Spain — the houses of worship are required to be located on side streets and to conduct their services in such a way as not to attract public attention; nor is any public effort to spread a religion other than Catholicism tolerated. In practice, I must add, they have been subjected to considerable harassment but in principle their situation is as I have described it.

I must confess that I do not see how one can mount a powerful argument against the Spanish arrangement from the rights of conscience alone. Granted, it would be inhuman and immoral to force a person to profess or to practice a religion in which he did not believe. It follows that therefore he should have the right to profess and practice the religion in which he does believe, within the limits which public order and morality allow. But does it follow that his conscience is violated if he is restrained from public efforts to persuade others to abandon their religion and adopt his?

For my part, I cannot see how one can derive from an analysis of the rights of the individual conscience such conclusions as that the state should be neutral as among different religions, or that all religions ought to be equal before the law or that everyone must have the same degree of freedom to propagate and spread his faith. Guarantees of the individual's right to follow his conscience in matters of religion are compatible, so far as I can see, with the existence of an established and specially privileged religion, such as is found in the Protestant kingdoms of Great Britain and Scandinavia. They are also compatible with restrictions on the individual's freedom to proselytize publicly, as is the case in Spain.

I am not, of course, advocating that other countries should follow the example either of Spain or of Scandinavia. I do think that one must have recourse to other principles than the rights of conscience alone, if one wants to prove them wrong.

Another, more practical argument in favor of religious liberty is taken from the requirements of the common good in a pluralist society. We owe the most authoritative statement of this argument to Pope Pius XII, in his allocution to the Italian Congress of Jurists on December 6, 1953 (*Catholic Mind*, LII [1954], 244 ff.).

In his allocution the Pope addressed himself to the question of a European Political Community which was then under consideration by the states which later formed the Common Market. One of the features of this projected international union was of particular interest to the Church. Pius XII stated the question which such a political union would pose for Catholics in these terms:

> Could a norm be established in a community of states, at least in certain circumstances, that the free exercise of a belief and of a religious or moral practice which possesses validity in one of the member states be not hindered by laws or coercive measures of the state throughout the entire territory of the community of nations? In other words, the question is raised whether in these circumstances *"non impedire"* or toleration is permissible, and whether consequently positive repression is not always a duty.

To answer this question, said Pius XII, two principles must be applied. The first is: "That which does not correspond to truth or to the norm of morality objectively has no right to exist, to spread or to be activated." Here the Pope insists on the superiority of truth over error and denies that a society has the right to regard them as equal. But the second norm which he lays down is this: "Failure to impede this [spread of error] with civil laws and coercive measures can nevertheless be justified in the interests of a higher and more general good." Therefore, Pius XII said: "The duty of repressing moral and religious error cannot be an ultimate norm of action. It must be subordinate to higher and more general norms, which in some circumstances permit, and even perhaps seem to indicate as the better policy, toleration of error in order to promote a greater good."

At first glance, Pius XII's allocution may look like a mere restatement of the distinction between thesis and hypothesis. He repeats, in different terms, the old principle that error has no rights and goes no further than to admit that under certain circumstances toleration of error may be permitted or may even seem to be the better policy.

Upon analysis, however, I believe that it will appear that Pius XII went considerably beyond advocating religious toleration as a policy of mere expediency. To bring this out, I shall make the following points.

1. It has often been pointed out that the phrase, error has no rights, is meaningless, since rights belong to persons, not to ideas, whether true or false. Pius XII, we must assume, was well aware of this. What he meant was that when a person is acknowledged to have the right to spread an error, the right does not derive from the error. It requires some justification other than the false doctrine itself.

2. He speaks of this "right," as the U. S. Constitution also does in the First Amendment, in legal and negative terms. He is not concerned immediately with a person's moral right to propagate his belief, but with his freedom from being impeded in his propaganda by civil laws and coercive measures. The right, therefore, which Pius XII has in mind is a legal right against government.

3. He finds the justification for granting and guaranteeing this right in a "higher and more general good." The good which he had especially in mind in his allocution to the Italian jurists was the common good of a community of nations. But his words would apply with equal force to the common good of a single nation. In our rapidly shrinking world, I think that they would apply also to the common good of the world group of nations. A world community cannot be said to exist at present. But, as John XXIII pointed out in *Pacem in Terris*, a worldwide common good is coming into being. One indication of it is that concepts of human rights are becoming internationalized today and there is a growing sense among men that certain basic norms of freedom are universal. It would not be stretching Pius XII's thought too far to say that the "higher and more general good" of the world permits or even requires universal religious freedom.

4. While Pius XII speaks of "the duty of repressing moral and religious error," he also says that it "cannot be an ultimate norm of action." It is a subordinate norm. It would thus appear dubious whether we can continue to speak of a state in which religious error is repressed as being the "thesis" and of a state which tolerates it as being in a situation of "hypothesis."

5. It is true that Pius XII spoke of toleration of error as being permitted for the sake of a greater good in "certain circumstances." But I think it a fair interpretation of his thought to say that the circumstances which he contemplated are likely to be permanent ones, insofar as any historical circumstances can be permanent. He certainly did not advocate tolerance as a temporary expedient, to be permitted until Catholics should be numerous enough to revoke it. Indeed, he does not seem to consider the question whether Catholics are the majority or the minority as being relevant to his discussion. He was talking about the constitution of a new society, a European Political Community, and the purpose of his allocution was to give reasons why Catholics could accept religious freedom as its basic law. His argument was derived from considerations of expediency, if you will, but it was an exalted and long-term expediency and not mere opportunism. The toleration of religious error is justified, Pius XII said, because the common good of society demands it.

There is still another argument in favor of freedom of religion which is derived, as I am convinced it should be, not from the rights of the individual conscience alone but from the nature of the state. One of the best exponents of this argument is Fr. John Courtney Murray, S.J.

Fr. Murray takes as his starting point the oft-cited statement of Pius XII in his Christmas Message of 1944: "In our times, in which the activity of the state is so vast and decisive, the democratic form of government appears to many as a natural demand imposed by reason itself." From this proposition, Fr. Murray reasons thus: if the Church can accept democracy as a legitimate form of government and even as a form which perhaps the natural law itself requires in our times, then surely the Church can and does accept all that is necessarily implicit in democracy. Among the principles inherent in the idea of democracy, religious liberty holds a high and necessary place.

Let me state the argument at some length in Fr. Murray's own words (the internal quotations are from Pius XII's Christmas Message of 1944):

There can in fact be no popular share in power, no political responsibility of rulers in their elective capacity to the people, no effective right of citizens "to express their own opinion on the duties and sacrifices that are imposed on them," and "not to be constrained to obey without having been heard," no set of conditions apt "to put the citizen in a continually better position to have a personal opinion and to express it and to enforce it in a manner that will contribute to the common good" — there can be none of these things without those constitutional means for the vindication of rights and interests and for the direction of the political process which are known as the democratic institutions — freedom of opinion, of association, of speech, of the press. These freedoms are therefore, by political necessity, included in the democratic concept of *libertas civilis;* they are part of the common good; their constitutional guarantee has in fact come to be part of the very definition of the democratic state. Without them it is not in fact possible for the human person to be "the bearer, the basis, and the end of social life," in a manner conformed to the demands of his dignity, as these demands present themselves to reason in the present state of social evolution. Moreover, it is now judged not politically possible or just to except out of the guarantee of these freedoms the freedom of religious association and a constitutional right to the free expression of religious opinion. Such an exception is not just; for it inevitably implies some violation of that political equality which all the citizens of a state may justly claim as a basic civic right. Such an exception is not politically possible; for as Sturzo has pointed out [*Church and State* (London, 1939), pp. 429, 527], in a judgment confirmed by all manner of political experience, all the democratic freedoms form an organic whole. Each is part of a system of liberty; all are coherent. As political institutions all the particular freedoms rest on the same general judgment — that the system as such is rational, necessary for the common good, related to the political realization of personal dignity — whatever may be the defects in the workings of the institutions. It is not therefore possible within this system to make exceptions without endangering the political system itself. Consequently, the historically realized concept of *libertas civilis* has come to include "religious liberty" in a sense as ample as the concept of civil liberty itself ("Contemporary Orientations of Catholic Thought on Church and State in the Light of History," *Theological Studies,* X [1949], pp. 182–183).

Fr. Murray's argument for religious liberty, like Pius XII's, is an argument from the common good, not from the antecedent rights of conscience. But Fr. Murray does not simply defend religious liberty as a toleration of error required by the common good in today's circumstances. He asserts that it is a constituent part of the common good of the democratic state. Wherever democracy is established, therefore, freedom of religion must be established, too.

The democratic state, his argument runs, cannot exist without the constitutional guarantee of certain rights. Freedom of religion, which means freedom of religious association and the free expression of religious opinion, must be among those rights. There are two reasons, according to Fr. Murray, why this is so. One is that, since the democratic liberties form a coherent whole, it is impossible to make an exception of religious liberty. The other is that, since the denial of freedom of religion would violate the political equality which citizens claim as a basic civic right, it would be unjust to withhold religious liberty from the list of guaranteed constitutional rights.

Fr. Murray's argument thus rests, it seems to me, on the premise that the democratic state is a political society of equals. The state must therefore regard its members as having an equal right to their religious beliefs, whatever they may be. The constitution of a democratic state does not assert that all religions are equal — the state is not competent to make that judgment — but that all citizens are equal and for that reason have an equal right to form religious associations and to express their religious beliefs.

This is a sound argument, I think. It is based ultimately, not on the separation of Church and state but on something far more fundamental, the *distinction* between the Church and the state — a distinction which the Catholic Church can claim to have invented. According to this distinction, which is as old as Christianity, the state is one society and the Church is quite another. The democratic state infers from this that membership in the political society is different from and independent of membership in the Church. For reasons derived from its own nature, the democratic state guarantees to its members an equal freedom of religion. Since the Church regards democracy as a rational and praiseworthy form of government, Fr. Murray concludes, the Church must regard democracy's constitutional freedom of religion as legitimate and acceptable.

Fr. Murray's argument was taken up and restated by the Catholic bishops of Tanganyika in a pastoral letter which they issued on the occasion of their country's independence in 1961 (*Catholic Mind*, LX [1962], pp. 59 ff.). In a paper already too long I cannot adequately summarize this magnificent pastoral letter. Rather than a summary, it deserves study in the original text as a candid statement of the Church's acceptance of democratic equality and religious liberty. For reasons which I shall not explain in detail here, it is also a penetrating and farsighted explanation of what the Church rightly claims from a pluralist society. One could wish that it were studied in the offices of such organizations as the American Civil Liberties Union, the American Jewish Congress, and Protestants and Other Americans United for Separation of Church and State.

To pare the Tanganyikan bishops' affirmation of religious liberty down to the barest essentials, we may note that they make the following points. First, the natural law asserts "the essential equality and dignity of the human being." From this it follows that "the same human and civic rights must be guaranteed to each and every member of every nationality, race or tribe living in any country." This means that "groups which follow a certain type of intellectual or spiritual tradition" have "the right to continued existence in that tradition, whether they be in the majority or the minority."

On the basis of these principles, the bishops describe the proper relation between religion and the state in these terms:

> The state must in a real way acknowledge God in its work, must recognize the belief of its citizens in God and their acceptance of the order of natural law.

The state has the duty of fostering religion.

However, the state has no rights over the religious convictions of its citizens. It must guarantee freedom of religion. This guarantee implies several things: first, that the state cannot force any citizen to practice a religion and perform the acts of a cult repugnant to his conscience; secondly, in acquitting itself of its responsibilities toward the public, the state must do so in the best interests of all and with complete impartiality as regards beliefs and religions; finally, it implies that no public servant has any right to show himself biased in favor of his co-religionists in the carrying out of his duties.

Finally, we must mention that the bishops firmly renounce any demand for special prerogatives from the state based on the Catholic Church's claim to be the one true Church. "We firmly believe," they say, "that the state will best help the Catholic Church by not forcing the conscience and by guaranteeing freedom of religion on the one hand, and by pursuing the common good on the other."

The position taken by the bishops of Tanganyika is one which is well adapted to a modern, democratic, and pluralistic society. It reflects a view which we can say is rapidly becoming the dominant one among Catholics, whether lay or clerical, who write on Church-State relations. We may be sure that it is a view which commends itself to many of the Fathers of the Ecumenical Council.

The Council, as I said at the beginning of this paper, has taken no formal action on this subject. But the matter has been set before it. On November 19, 1963, Bishop Emile de Smedt of Bruges (Belgium) gave a lengthy address introducing Chapter 5, entitled *"De Libertate Religiosa,"* of the schema on ecumenism. In the course of this speech he explained the concept of religious liberty contained in the chapter and the reasons why the Secretariat for Promoting Christian Unity, in whose name he spoke, urged the Council to adopt it as the Church's official position.

Without attempting to summarize all that is in Bishop de Smedt's address (or *relatio,* as it is officially called), I shall state what seem to be its essential affirmations. To begin with, it clears away several false notions of religious liberty which the draft chapter does not intend to propose or defend: religious indifferentism, laicism, doctrinal relativism and something which it calls dilettantistic pessimism. The religious liberty which it propounds is, positively, "the right of the human person to the free exercise of religion according to the dictates of his conscience. Negatively, it is immunity from all external force in his personal relations with God, which the conscience of man vindicates to itself."

The chapter on religious liberty, Bishop de Smedt made plain, "asserts that each and every man, who follows his conscience in religious matters, has a *natural* right to true and authentic religious liberty" (italics added). It proposes that the Council solemnly demand freedom of religion "for the whole human family, for all religious groups, for each human person whether his conscience be sincere and true or sincere and false concerning faith, provided only that he sincerely follow the dictate of conscience."

Nothing less is asserted here than a universal natural right of all men to freedom to follow their consciences in matters of religion. The reason why this is a natural right is also explained: "The human person, endowed with conscience and free activity, since he can fulfill the will of God only as the divine law is perceived through the dictate of conscience, can obtain his ultimate end only by prudently forming the judgment of conscience and by faithfully carrying out its dictate."

In other words, man's first obligation is to obey God. But he can do God's will only as it is known to him, and his awareness of God's will is his conscience. He must therefore follow his conscience in order to obey God, even though his conscience should be objectively wrong, that is, mistaken about what God really wants. It is this obligation that is the source of the right to freedom of religion. As Bishop de Smedt says further on in his address: "From this absolute dependence of man upon God there flows every right and duty of man to claim for himself and for others true religious liberty. For man is subjectively bound to worship God according to the sincere dictate of his own conscience because objectively he is absolutely dependent upon God."

It is curious that Bishop de Smedt did not cite the classical Christian text: "It is necessary to obey God rather than men" (Acts 5:29). The Church has always relied on this forthright declaration of independence by the Apostle St. Peter to justify her freedom from any human authority in preaching the Gospel of Christ. It seems to me that Chapter 5 of the schema on ecumenism represents a development of Catholic doctrine only to this extent: what the Church has always vindicated for herself and for her members she is now asked to recognize as a right inherent in every human conscience provided only that it is in sincere submission to the will of God, even though it may be objectively mistaken.

That is the central affirmation of the chapter on religious liberty. Bishop de Smedt did not explain in detail what practical conclusions the chapter draws from it. Since the text of the chapter has not been published, we do not know. I am informed, how reliably I cannot say, that it states that religious liberty would be infringed, not only by the infliction of civil penalties for one's religious belief, but also by the denial of social or civil equality for that reason. If so, it is a sweeping assertion of the equality of all religions before the law, not because all religions are equally true but because all men have an equal right to freedom of religion. I have already stated my reasons for being skeptical whether one can draw so broad a conclusion from the rights of conscience alone.

Bishop de Smedt did say, however, that the chapter recognizes that there must be some restrictions on the exercise of the rights of conscience: "if a human person carries out the dictate of his conscience by external acts, there is danger of violating the rights and duties of another or of others. Since man is a social being and since in the human family men are subject to error and to sin, the conflict of rights and the conflict of duties cannot always be avoided." Hence, he said, "it is evident that the right and duty to manifest externally the dictate of conscience is not unlimited, but can be and at times must be tempered and regulated for the common good."

At this point it is relevant to cite certain criticisms of the chapter on religious liberty which Fr. John Courtney Murray made in the November 30, 1963, number of *America*. It is perfectly true, he said, that "the exercise of the right to religious freedom, since it takes place publicly and in society, is subject to some legitimate restrictions." But to allow these restrictions to be imposed by public authority in the name of the common good carries with it the danger of a denial of men's rights for the sake of political expediency.

This criticism is directed against the text of the draft chapter which Fr. Murray, as a *peritus* or expert consultant of the Council, had naturally read. He found Bishop de Smedt's address or *relatio* more satisfactory and remarked:

> The *relatio* makes clear that the primary element in the common good consists in the legal protection and promotion of the whole order of personal rights and freedoms which are proper to the human persons as such. Therefore the *relatio* also makes clear that an infringement of the personal rights of man, including notably his right to religious freedom, cannot be justified by an appeal to the common good. Such an infringement of personal rights would be a violation of the common good itself.

We note in this passage Fr. Murray's concern, which we saw earlier, to incorporate men's fundamental rights into the common good itself. Obviously, since the common good is common, it must rest upon some philosophy which either is or can be the object of a consensus among citizens and not on every individual's own conception of what his rights are. No society can let everyone regulate his social actions by his conscience alone. Yet, on the other hand, if personal freedom is to be protected against majority tyranny, society must recognize that the safeguarding of the rights of the human person is a basic part of the very object for which society exists, namely the common good and general welfare.

Fr. Murray also said in his *America* article that another principle, of a juridical and constitutional nature, is required to complete the affirmation of the right to religious freedom in the chapter on religious liberty. That is the incompetence of government as judge or arbiter in the field of religious truth. He said:

> Government is a secular authority whose competence is limited to the temporal and terrestrial affairs of men who must live together in justice, peace and freedom. Government would therefore act *ultra vires* (beyond its scope) if it were to undertake to judge this religion to be true and that religion to be false. Government would be acting even more evidently *ultra vires* if it were to enforce upon citizens, by the medium of law, any kind of theological judgment; if, that is, it were to assert by law that a particular religion — say, the Catholic religion — ought to be the religion of the national community.

This point, too, seems well taken to me. With all the respect we owe to the individual conscience, I do not think we can adequately define its rights in society by mere analysis of the individual person's obligation to follow that conscience. We need a political philosophy that propounds a sound concept of the common good and of the nature and functions of the state.

All of this, of course, is speculation on what the Council may accept and make its own. We must remember that, up to the present, the Council has done nothing on the subject of freedom of religion. But if the Council were to adopt the substance of the Secretariat for Promoting Christian Unity's draft chapter on religious liberty and the Holy Father should approve it, we would then have the most authoritative statement of the Church's commitment to religious freedom for which one could wish.

Surely Catholics today must wish for such a commitment. To quote Fr. Murray's *America* article once again, "The question today is whether the Church should extend her pastoral solicitude beyond her own boundaries and assume an active patronage of the freedom of the human person, who was created by God as His image, who was redeemed by the blood of Christ, who stands today under a massive threat to everything that human dignity

and personal freedom mean." As the human race moves into an ever more tightly organized world, there is no posture our Holy Mother the Church could more gracefully adopt than that of universal patroness of the dignity and freedom of the human person.

WALTER J. BURGHARDT, S.J.

MARY: OBSTACLE TO REUNION?

THE precise problem that this essay confronts may be phrased in a single question: Is the Catholic vision of Mary, is Catholic veneration of the Virgin, an obstacle to the union of the churches? On broad lines there are three answers to this question, three positions, three attitudes. There are two extremes and a middle.

One extreme I shall call the left. Where it exists, it is normally a Protestant position. What is its basic affirmation? Mary is an insuperable obstacle to unity. Unless the Catholic Church retracts her Mariological past, unless she checks her Mariological present, unless she gives evident sign that her Mariological future will be different, unity is impossible. Yesterday's Assumption must be retracted; today's worship must be disowned; and tomorrow's coredemption must never come. As long as Marian theology and devotion remain on their contemporary path, Catholicism is in violent contradiction to Christ.

This is a serious obstacle, and the obstacle is insuperable. Why insuperable? Because, on the issue of Mary, Roman Catholicism (1) stands in direct contradiction to the Gospel, (2) will not change her stand, and (3) cannot change without ceasing to be herself. This is idolatry, but Romanism is stuck with it. All Protestantism can do is continue to protest it, as she protests all idolatry.

In sum, an insuperable division: on the one hand, idolatry — on principle; on the other hand, protest — on principle.

The other extreme I shall call the right. Where it exists, it is invariably a Catholic position. What is its basic affirmation? Mary cannot possibly be an obstacle to unity. After all, she is the Mother of Christ, and her traditional role ever since Nazareth has been to lead men *to* her Son, not away from Him. And how can you say too much of her, when the saints have sung *"De Maria numquam satis"* — you can never say enough about Mary? In point of fact, she preserves unity, for she more than anyone else destroys what is not genuinely Christian. Does not the Church chant of her on the feast of the Annunciation: "Rejoice, Virgin Mary: thou alone hast overthrown all heresies"?

In sum, no obstacle: Mary *is* no obstacle because she *cannot* be an obstacle.

I submit that these two positions are extreme positions; and because they are extreme, each betrays the truth in its own way. The right-wing approach — Mary is no obstacle — is overly optimistic; such optimism is not justified by the facts; it stems from sheer theory, to the neglect of the existential situation. The left-wing approach — Mary is an insuperable obstacle — is overly pessimistic; such pessimism is not justified by the facts; it stems, in some measure at least, from misunderstanding, from a misreading of the evidence.

I suggest, therefore, that the truth lies in the middle. My thesis is: the Catholic vision of Mary — theology — and the Catholic veneration of Mary — devotion — *is* an obstacle to the union of the churches; but the obstacle is *not* insuperable. What is imperative here is understanding — on four levels; and these four facets of understanding form the four points of my paper.

First, Catholics must understand why Protestants reject the Catholic vision and veneration of Mary. Second, Protestants must understand why Catholics see Mary and honor her as they do. Third, Catholics must re-examine their present position on Mary — mind and heart, theology and devotion — to discover if, and to what extent, they have given Protestants cause for legitimate concern. Fourth, Protestants must re-examine their present position on Mary — mind and heart, theology and devotion — to discover if, and to what extent, that position does injustice to God and to His Christ.

I

First, then, Catholics must understand why Protestants reject the Catholic vision and veneration of Mary. What lies behind the Protestant reaction and rejection? Why is it that, in the face of Catholic devotion to Mary, Protestants are offended, feel uncomfortable, sound bitter? How is it that "Mariolatry" has entered every dictionary as an epithet of abuse, a Protestant characterization of Roman Catholicism?

There is a facile Catholic answer: Protestants are prejudiced. With their mothers' milk they imbibe a warped view of Catholicism, a distortion of Catholic devotion. The Protestant pulpit intensifies the image, contrasting the Catholic queen of heaven with the Gospel maid of Nazareth. Secular education consummates the caricature, tracing the Catholic veneration of the Virgin back to its roots in the mother goddesses of paganism. Little wonder that the Protestant suspects our Lady, avoids her, dislikes her: he is biased, and his bias stems from crass ignorance.

I do not deny that there are prejudiced Protestants; Catholics have no monopoly on bias. I do not doubt that in some instances Protestants dislike Mary because they dislike Catholics. But the point I make is this: thinking Protestants shy away from Mary, reject the Catholic vision and veneration of Mary, on theological grounds. Their rejection has its roots in their grasp of the Gospel, in their understanding of Christ and His revelation.

On the matter of Mary, the Protestant reaction centers around three ideas: mediation, holiness, divinity.

First, mediation. Scripture speaks of one mediator between God and man. That mediator is Jesus Christ. There is no mediator besides Him. He is the one only bridge between the all-holy God and sinful man. Through Him, and through Him alone, sinful man has access to the Father; through Him, and through Him alone, the grace of God comes down to man. This unique position of Christ Catholic theology threatens. As the ecumenical scholar Gregory Baum has put it:

"The Protestant fears that the Catholic devotion to Mary intro-

duces the human into a realm where the human does not count.
He believes that by trusting in Mary's merits or in her interces-
sion the Catholic puts his hope in man and not in God, and is
on the verge of humanizing a divine religion. The Protestant
fears that the Catholic is in danger of forgetting the very centre
of the Gospel — the doctrine, namely, that salvation is the gift
of God, and that it is available only in the name of Christ."[1]

Second, holiness. As the Protestant understands the Gospel,
God alone is holy — God and His Son, our Lord Jesus Christ.
Not man. "For the Protestant the whole of human life is inextri-
cably involved in limitation, ambiguity and sin."[2] Oh yes, man
can, with God's grace, keep from breaking God's law openly,
obviously. He can avoid adultery and idolatry, shun murder and
hate. But selfishness is so intimately woven into the fabric of
sinful man that even in our good actions a certain self-seeking is
inevitable, inescapable. Even well on his way to God, man remains a sinner, a sinful creature, in ceaseless need of God's mercy.

But Catholics, in their theology of Mary, in their veneration of
the Virgin, lift her above the human situation. We give her, from
the first moment of her existence, a holiness which is not man's
to possess in his mortal frame; we set her beyond the need, each
moment, of the Saviour's mercy. This sort of holiness, the Protestant affirms, stands in flagrant contradiction to the Gospel.

Third, divinity. The Protestant is convinced that Roman Catholicism has raised our Lady to the level of divinity. Oh, he knows
that we deny the accusation. He knows what we *say* about
divinity, our doctrine on the Trinity. There is but one God,
triune, Father, Son, and Holy Spirit. And Mary is a creature, a
human being, a woman, fashioned by God, utterly dependent
on God.

But, he insists, what we affirm with one side of our mouth we
deny with the other. We say she is human, yet we give her
powers which are divine. She helped redeem the world; she

---

[1] G. Baum, "Protestants Look at Mary," *Furrow* 13, no. 8 (Aug., 1962), p.
456. My first point owes much to this discerning article (*ibid.*, pp. 455–461).
[2] *Ibid.*, p. 456.

mediates between God and man; she dispenses God's grace. We call her "our life, our sweetness, and our hope." In this "we transgress the limits of true biblical religion by ascribing to man, to little man, what belongs only and exclusively to God, the sole author of power and mercy."[3]

We say that Mary is human, yet we grace her with qualities which are God's alone. She is immaculate; she knows not concupiscence; the slightest stain of sin is far from her; she is a mirror of holiness. You may *call* her human, the Protestant says, but all this *makes* her divine.

Here, too — the Protestant insists — here too, as in so much else, Catholicism imperils an important Christian experience: the direct encounter of the soul with God. Catholic theology destroys the directness of that encounter; it is constantly inserting someone or something between the soul and God: a priest, a sacrament, the Church — and now Mary.

Such, in summary, is the position of thinking Protestants. Catholics may justifiably deny that these charges are valid; they may not justifiably trace them to bad will, to hatred, to an un-Christian spirit. Quite the contrary: the impressive thing about these protests is that they stem from a concern for Christ, from a fear that His uniqueness is being jeopardized. Can a Catholic quarrel with such a concern?

II

My second point: Protestants must understand why Catholics see Mary and honor her as they do. What explains the Catholic vision and veneration of Mary? There is a facile Protestant answer: Catholics have abandoned the Gospel. Over the centuries Roman Catholicism has moved farther and farther away from primitive Christianity, from the centrality of Christ, from the Gospel idea of redemption. The first century was the age of Jesus; the twentieth is the age of Mary. Bethlehem was the cradle of Christology; Rome is the manger of Mariolatry.

I do not deny that there are Catholics who do not know Christ

---

[3] *Ibid.*, p. 457.

and His redemptive work; Protestants have no monopoly on ignorance. I do not doubt that in some instances, in some Catholics, superstition has triumphed over religion. But the point I make is this: the Catholic vision of Mary, Catholic veneration of Mary, is not an unthinking thing. Its basis is a serious, sincere theology. It has its roots in the Catholic grasp of the Gospel, in the Catholic understanding of Christ and His revelation.

Gregory Baum has put it pithily: "We affirm that the Catholic vision of the redemption Christ has wrought is really different from that of classical Protestantism. We believe that the grace of Christ is so powerful, vital, and so well adapted to our human nature that it elevates us, makes us co-operators with God in the work of our salvation. We are convinced, moreover, that this call to become co-operators with God in Christ is authentically biblical.

"The transformation in grace takes place in every Christian soul, but it takes place in a much more intense way in the *Church,* the community in which Christ remains in the world, and in *Mary,* the embodiment of redeemed humanity."[4]

In the light of this conception of redemption, what does authentic Catholic theology say to the three-pronged Protestant protest: Christ alone is mediator; God alone is holy; a human Mary has been made divine?

First, one mediator. "Jesus Christ is the unique mediator. In Him, and in Him alone, God has given us all riches and the fullness of grace. But precisely because His grace is so powerful, Christ makes all who live in Him sharers in His own mediation. There is no mediator or mediatrix apart from Christ or outside of Him. *In Him,* however, every Christian is an instrument of divine salvation for others; and in Him, due to the close relationship to her Son, Mary is a mediatrix in an altogether special way."[5]

This mediation of Mary, the Catholic insists, does not detract from the power of Christ, minimize His mediation. Quite the contrary: it exalts His power, heightens His mediation. It is *in*

---

[4] *Ibid.,* p. 458.
[5] *Ibid.*

Him and *through* Him that Mary exercises what mediation is hers. And it is *from* Him that her power stems, from the blood that ransomed the world, the blood that redeemed *her*.

Second, holiness. The Catholic recognizes that God is supremely holy, sovereignly holy, incomparably holy; there is no holiness on earth or in heaven that touches His. But the Catholic insists that genuine holiness, a share in God's holiness, is possible to men. We know it is possible if only because this human holiness, utter freedom from sin, found its perfection in the human nature of Christ. And nearest of humankind to this perfection of Christ is the perfection of His mother.

Once again, "holy Mary" does not detract from the holiness of God, make Him less unique. In fact, it heightens God's holiness; for human holiness is a share in infinite holiness; it is God's self-giving, out of sheer mercy; it reveals, more vividly than words, the power of God's grace, which can transform a sinful creature, without prior merit, from an image of Adam to an image of Christ.

Third, divinity. The Catholic rejects the protest that the prerogatives of Mary lift her to the level of the divine. She mediates, yes, but not in her own right, only in and through the one mediator. She is holy, yes, but with the holiness of Christ. Mediation and holiness, each is a gift to her, a gift which powerfully illustrates the power of God, the transforming power of His grace.

And if the Protestant counters with his deathblow, his *coup de grâce*, his Sunday punch, "All well and good, but it still remains true that you have forsaken Scripture: you will not find this in the word of God," the Catholic theologian is not seriously stunned. He knows that this objection, this protest, simply takes the problem of Mary back to an issue even more basic: How does the Christian know what Scripture means? When Christ our Lord affirms, "The Father and I are one," how do I know what that oneness involves? When the angel addresses Mary, "Hail, Mary, highly favored" (or, as the Douay version has it, "full of grace"), how do I know what that divine favor implies?

Contemporary Protestant scholarship and traditional Catholic

theology agree on this: Scripture is not self-explanatory; it needs
interpretation; and the interpretation must take place within the
Church, by the Church. And here you confront the basic issue
in the ecumenical movement, the most divisive of all issues:
What is the Church? The question cannot be answered here;
but the question must be put.

The Catholic agrees with the Protestant that the Church is the
people of God; but he insists that this people is, by divine intent,
a structured reality, where the various members have various
functions; where the structure involves not only humility before
God but also authority under God, not only learning the word
of God but teaching the word of God, not only being sanctified
by Christ but sanctifying with and through Christ. He admits,
with St. Paul, that in this structured Body of Christ "the head
cannot say to the foot, 'I have no need of you'"; but he insists
that the head *can* and *must* say to the foot, "This is what you
must believe, because it is God's word; this is what you must
do, because it is God's will."

What I have said in this second point is not a refutation of
Protestant objections; it does not destroy, once and for all, the
Protestant protest. I have indicated only that the Catholic vision
of Mary is based on a Catholic vision of redemption, that it is
profoundly theological, that it is not necessarily unscriptural, that
like the Protestant protest it too is motivated by a loving concern
for Christ.

III

My third point: Catholics must examine their present position
on Mary — mind and heart, theology and devotion — to discover
if, and to what extent, they have given Protestants cause for legitimate concern. This — in the context of the ecumenical movement,
the search for unity — this is the task of every Catholic: not only
the Pope as he presides over an ecumenical council, but the
pious laywoman too as she whispers her beads during the Consecration of the Mass.

First, on the level of theology. For all too long, the theological treatise on Mary was unjustifiably separated from the theological treatise on Christ — as though the prerogatives of the mother could possibly be considered in isolation from the person and work of her Son. In our lifetime this tendency has been remarkably reversed. More specifically, some theologians have given a bad impression by pushing insistently for papal or conciliar definition of Marian prerogatives which do not seem to have reached sufficient theological maturity. Thus, an intimate adviser of Pope Pius XII writes that "on the subject of the titles of 'mediatrix' and 'coredemptrix,' Pius XII, a few weeks before his death and just after the Mariological Congress at Lourdes, said that both matters were too unclear and too unripe; that he had consciously and deliberately, throughout his pontificate, avoided taking up any positive attitude toward them, preferring to leave them to free theological discussion. It was not his intention to alter this attitude."[6] I do not claim that these titles and the doctrines they embody are unjustified; I would simply ask that theologians imitate the prudence of Pius XII, his theological insight.

Second, on the level of the liturgy. Here, for examination of conscience, I reproduce the words of Cardinal Montini (now Pope Paul VI) to the Liturgical Study Week at Vicenza: "The liturgy is not only a means of teaching us dogmatic truth; it is also a school of holiness and one of the principal means of uniting our souls with Christ. Hence it is to be hoped that the work of this Congress will be devoted especially to this aspect of Marian liturgy. This will, where necessary, bring devotion to the most blessed Virgin back to its pure goal, so that it recovers its real function of bringing souls to Jesus by the speediest, most total and most loving transformation possible of the old man into the new man of righteousness and Christian holiness. Any other form of Marian piety, insufficiently orientated in this direction,

---

[6] R. Leiber, S.J., in *Stimmen der Zeit*, reprinted in *Civitas* 14 (1958), 81; tr. in H. Küng, *The Council, Reform and Reunion*, tr. C. Hastings (New York, 1961), pp. 126–127.

would thereby necessarily show itself as deficient and as displeasing to the heavenly Mother."[7]

Third, on the level of popular piety. I mean those books of piety, those popular devotions, those Marian pilgrimages, those sodalities, those sermons on Mary, those statues of Mary which seem to isolate her from her Son. This is not a condemnation of devotion to our Lady; such devotion is an integral part of Catholic living. It does mean, however, that an examination of conscience is in order — for every Catholic. In my spiritual life, is Mary genuinely a way to Jesus, or has the mother displaced her Son? Is the Rosary a fetish, or is it what it ought to be: meditation on the life and death of Christ, on redemption and its transforming power? In a word, is Christ still the center of my life?

IV

My fourth and final point: Protestants must re-examine their present position on Mary — mind and heart, theology and devotion — to discover if, and to what extent, that position does injustice to God and His Christ. On this point the young German theologian Hans Küng has a splendid passage in his impressive book *The Council, Reform and Reunion*. He is making the point that in Marian doctrine and devotion men may sin not only by excess but by neglect. And he goes on to say:

". . . as we do not spare ourselves in our examination of conscience, so our Protestant brethren cannot spare themselves either; they must ask themselves some such questions as these: What do we [Protestants] make of the numerous Marian passages in Scripture? Something positive and creative in theology and in piety, or only something critical and defensive? Where do we stand in regard to Luther's undeniable Marian piety? Can we really describe anti-Marianism as a requirement of 'reform'? What are the roots of the anti-Marianism in *modern* Protestantism? Is it ultimately anti-Roman? Are Protestant Christians included or

---

[7] Quoted by H. Schütte, *Um die Wiedervereinigung im Glauben* (2nd ed., Essen, 1959), p. 148; tr. in H. Küng, *op. cit.*, p. 127.

not in 'All generations shall call me blessed'? Is calling her blessed to be done only silently, only shamefacedly, only peripherally, only privately? Is it only to be taught (and often not even that), or to be lived as well? Can we raise our voices in praise of Christ without also raising them in praise of her who spoke the decisive *fiat* to Christ? Can we be Christian without — though in a different way — being Marian too? ... Considering how often it took centuries to plumb the depths of scriptural meaning, is it not possible that here too there were precious treasures lying hidden for quiet meditation and prayer to discover? Can there, finally, be any reunion in Christ which would leave the mystery of Mary to one side? Do we not here again need the undiminished Gospel, given its undiminished value and brought out into the full light of day?

"Once again [Küng concludes], it is only reform from *both* sides that can help us."[8]

I have made four major points in this presentation: (1) the Catholic must understand the roots of the Protestant protest; (2) the Protestant must understand the roots of the Catholic position; (3) the Catholic must re-examine his position for the excess therein; (4) the Protestant must re-examine his position for the neglect therein.

If and when this is done, will all be sweetness and light? Will the Marian crisis that divides us disappear? I do not know; you see, the theology of Mary is too intimately linked to a more fundamental problem, what is the Church?, ever to be solved in isolation from it. What such examination *will* achieve is this: (1) the area of disagreement will be significantly narrowed, for false issues will be discarded, real issues recognized; (2) Protestants should come to see that Marian theology and devotion, when shorn of accidental excess, is motivated by a true concern for Christ; (3) the Protestant theologian may eventually recognize that the Catholic vision of our Lady is not necessarily unscriptural. If this is achieved, we shall have come a long way toward oneness.

---

[8] Küng, *op. cit.*, pp. 127–128.

ECUMENICAL CATHOLICITY*

IN HIS book, *Insights*, Martin Buber writes: What weight do all misguided discussions on God's essence and operations have when contrasted with the one truth that all men, who have addressed God, have the same God in mind? Let us carry this thought over to historic Christianity: How significant are the plurality and division when contrasted with the one truth that all who have been called by Christ in faith have Him in mind? The ecumenical meetings and endeavors made by Protestants and Catholics have reminded us that in spite of the deep differences that exist among Christians, they all want to be loyal to the same truth (L. Newbigin).

Divisive differences no longer arise from the old controversial questions concerning the justification of man (the grace of God before and in all human endeavors), nor from questions concerning the relation between Scripture and Tradition (the apostolic revelation stated in Holy Scripture as the fundamental norm of all later revelations, and of all legitimate expressions of ecclesiastical life). Neither do they lie in the inner relation between faith and sacrament, in regard to the Eucharist as participating in the One Sacrifice of Jesus Christ, and bearing the imprint of the transfigured Lord (as "substance" under the sacramental veils), nor in the ordering of the spirit to a proper authority, of the community to its pastor. Within recent decades, by means of research in biblical theology, and as a result of ecumenical declarations, all these

---

* Reprinted from *Cross Currents*, Winter, 1960. (Translated by Gerard Farley.)

questions have led, on the Protestant side, to a re-examination of old positions, and to a positive evaluation of Catholic doctrine — and simultaneously, to a rectification of our corresponding counter-Reformation attitudes. The divisive factor in ecclesiastical life today is rooted in the question: what is the Church?

In the first place we should mention the idea of the Church prevalent in Eastern Orthodoxy. The "sobornost," the fraternal solidarity of the independent episcopal churches, regards unity as a mystical ideal without a divinely placed center in the Papacy. In itself, this mystical magnetism would appear as a type of bridge between the Roman Catholic and the Protestant ideas of the Church; it falls short, however, of biblical unity. As Newman remarked, "Each of these churches is a replica of the others, and in regard to its divine prerogatives, each is as much 'the complete Church' as all taken together: each is equal to the other, each independent and fully endowed with powers of the Spirit. All of this, however, rests upon a denial of a Church divinely founded and commissioned, a divinely organized totality. And this is a position unknown to Holy Scripture."

A second explanation of ecclesiastical unity starts with historical separations and seeks to reconcile itself with given conditions. It makes a virtue out of necessity, a type of ideal position wherein one either escapes from historical forms to "an invisible church of love" or into the dilemma of a church composed of many similar branches. The "invisible Church" is no longer maintained by theologians who believe in the authenticity of the Bible. The "branch theory," developed by Anglican theologians in the past century, was rejected by Leo XIII and again by Pius XI. The Anglicans themselves now take a somewhat more sober view of it. Newbigin says: "The unity of the Church is not a union with friends chosen by us; it is, rather, the Unity specified by Christ Himself. For this reason I can view the image of unity in the sense of a confederation only as an error . . . for it offers unity without repentance."

The idea which the Anglo-Saxon wing of world ecumenism has

in mind today represents an essential step ahead when contrasted with this happily optimistic dream of a federal Church: "Catholicity from the (historically formed) fragments of the apostolic tradition" is what W. Nichols calls it. According to this view, the Church of the apostles has suffered severe historical disturbances. Instead of a *Catholica* we have a battlefield made up of a huge Christian arena, in which differing and mutually estranged groups of men build their divided chapels or pavilions out of the relics of a Holy Cathedral. "Christ in His totality is hidden (latent) in each church fragment and only in a united church will he be revealed (patent)" says O. Tomkins.

Whether influenced by these writings or not, the fact remains that Protestant theologians in Germany are very close to this basic position in their most recent writings. We are concerned with several important movements inspired by a desire for unity among the churches, which, in contrast with world ecumenism, views discussions with Roman Catholics as the most pressing task of Christian consciousness in our country. They have banded into the "Michaelsbrudershaft" and in the "Sammlung," and have produced a whole series of works with the object of community: *Credo ecclesiam* (1955), *Die Katholizität der Kirche* (1957), and *Katholische Reformation* (1958). The two groups led by K. B. Ritter, W. Stählin, and H. Asmussen with their lay and theologian friends, though numerically small, represent a leaven within German Protestantism. They do not consider the conditions of union with Rome as given; rather they hold that since the convulsion of the Reformation, and by means of the consciousness initiated at the Council of Trent, the Catholic Church has risen above the negative polemic in which the Reformation was enmeshed. These serious attitudes toward the present appearance of the papal Church have not been unmeaning for theologians of Ecumenical Catholicity — rather they voice a Protestant self-probing and an invitation for a corresponding penitential preparation in the Catholic Church. Surely, it is our responsibility to listen to this invitation.

The editors of the writings I have mentioned did not expect complete agreement from the Catholic side. But the statement from an influential place that it was the old "branch-theory" came as a surprise to them. The preface of Asmussen and Stählin to the book *The Catholicity of the Church* was used as evidence for this interpretation. "We believe that the divided members of the One Holy Catholic and Apostolic Church are being moved towards each other not only through their *diaspora* existence in a non-Christian world, but also through their own inner history. The future of the whole Christian church cannot be thought of without a renewed and deepened relationship between the divided church bodies." Then there is Stählin's statement at the beginning of his article: "The proper relationship of the divided churches, especially of the two great branches of western Christendom, is a vital question not only for the Christian church itself . . . but also for the preservation and care of the total inheritance which we in Europe and the entire West have to administer." Does the idea of a federated church lie in these words? The authors speak of "Christian churches" as is the custom in modern phraseology; the interpretation of this phrase depends upon the total context wherein it is found. A very well-known Catholic theologian speaks of "the mysterious rent which has separated the Church for centuries," but it would be hard for anyone reading it in context to interpret this as "the branch-theory." These writers are not speaking, in an abstract world of ideas, of the various parts whose sum would for the first time constitute the whole Church. They do not speak of a tree with many branches, whose very plurality belongs to the life and fruitfulness of the Church. They are, rather, talking about something entirely different — of the notorious fact that Christianity is split in its historical development. Subscribers to the "branch-theory" are reassured by this fact. The prophets of Ecumenical Catholicity are deeply disturbed by it, because this historical reality contradicts the idea and mission of the Church, and they are, consequently, calling loudly for a consideration of Unity. I felt obliged to ask the writers themselves — one orally, the other in writing, about their attitudes. Asmussen said: "a gross misunderstanding!" Stählin wrote me: "If you understand by the 'branch-theory' that the differing church bodies are related to each other as are the branches of a tree, I do not share this concept at all and I cannot understand how anyone could come to the conclusion that I do. At the same time I would not contest the fact that this theory has a kernel of truth in it; however, it cannot express the awareness of culpable division and of passionate responsibility for the unity of the Church." Thus the discussion is about the empirically culpable origin and presence of a divided church and not of the proper variety of development within the One Church. Furthermore we are not speaking of the Church as an abstract concept; we speak of it rather in its historical existence. Christ lives in the history of His body; the Church is made up of men in space and time — of men who are sinners, but who through the Spirit of Christ and the gifts of grace are made holy. For centuries now the crime of division lies over all Christianity. It is this that the authors of Ecumenical Catholicity are talking about. They have gained from us the impression that we, forced by historical awareness, are ready to acknowledge a co-culpability for the emergence of the split, but that we have not drawn the *de facto* conclusions from it. Instead, in our self-assurance of being the true children of Abraham, we have expected reflection and repentance only from others, without reviewing our part in the affair. In a discussion in Richard Bauman's *Rock of the World*, K. B. Ritter (certainly no enemy of the Catholic Church) says that the situation is apparently not hopeless, because the Catholic Church explains itself as essentially an apostolic authority. The only question is: "How does this apostolic authority understand itself? Does it regard its spiritual authority as given once and for all (unconditionally) and totally at its disposition, or as bound to the resurrected Lord and His Spirit? Does it realize that an authority is recognized in the measure to which it exercises itself in sacrificial service to the gospel and in the spirit of love, and is it thus prepared at any time to be called back to obedience to Christ? The dogmatic difference between Protestant and Roman theology is, according to Protestants, that what constitutes Divine Law in the Church is not free from biblical criticism and thus from self-examination and penitence."

Here we are actually at the core of the Church question. But before we go into the question of the promise, and the problem of authority and its spiritual application, a reflection on the historical reasons for the split is necessary. ("Knowledge of the different confessions must always be historically oriented," says H. Jedin.) An obscuring of the biblical idea of the Church arose through lack of clarity concerning the extent and limits of the Reformation, as well as through the overall disruption of spiritual authority and the worldliness of the Renaissance papacy. The call for a council should have been made; that it was not made in the ensuing years was largely due to the hesitation of the Roman curia. Had it not hesitated so long through fear of unwanted reforms enforced by a council, everything would have taken a different turn (at least as far as human reckoning goes) and there would have been no split. The later refusal of the Protestants to respond to the bull calling them to the Council of Trent in 1537 was, in view of the divided purposes of the Protestant theologians, "a political decision carried out by princes and magistrates" (Jedin). The division thus set a precedent which speaks harshly for the members of the Kingdom of God. Quite simply there was a growth away from each other, and all who followed inherited this tradition. On one side was the Catholic tradition and on the other the Protestant, and people were members of one or the other because they were so born and raised. In other words, the historical separation and division of Christianity by political powers into two different life-streams did not result in the same Christian content remaining untarnished in both of them. Objectively speaking the fullness of Christian being is present only in the Church which preserves the authority of the bishops and of the papacy. It is, however, also true that Protestant Christianity carries with it from its origins the well-springs of life, whose spirit is that of the One Church.

We must work for only one thing: that is, to heal the broken unity through mutual reflection on the apostolic inheritance, and to draw nearer to "perfect unity." If each confession wanted to glorify its inheritance at the expense of the others, it would amount to a deepening of unrest and would mean not listening to Christ. It is both truthful and in conformity with the command of the Lord to recognize the historically continuing division as involving mutual guilt, and in the spirit of Christian repentance "to avoid everything which can reasonably offend the other" (P. Ch. Boyer, Rome) and, for the sake of Christ, to do all that can be done for unity. The representatives of Ecumenical Catholicity have given me personally a deep impression of their moral and theological work for unity — and indeed precisely in relation to the crucial position of the Church, the apostolic succession of the See of Peter. But they do not expect us to act like the "holy possessors," as if we had nothing to contribute, as if we were a pure likeness of the apostolic Church.

In regard to the succession to authority, the New Testament uses its familiar words for office (*arché* and *exousía*), evidently because of their conceptual proximity to "lordship" or "power of disposal," when it is speaking of the political realm and the realm of the synagogue. They are never used in an ecclesiastical sense. In this context the word *diakonía* is used, i.e., service to the people of God in responsibility to the Lord and in the spirit of brotherhood. On this point both Catholic and Protestant exegetes are unanimous. With this purpose in mind the apostles appointed "shepherds" to the communities who, in their turn, could pass on their particular responsibilities to worthy men of good reputation, or even to worthy men proposed by the community. Those men who had been installed by others, through the holy signs of the laying on of hands and the call of the spirit, were then called "those established by the Holy Spirit," and so form "from the very beginning, for all time, the connecting links which come from eternity into time" (K. H. Schelkle). The liturgical prayers of consecration in both the West and the East show that the post-apostolic church was well aware of this idea of "holy authority." It was not buried in the following centuries, but rather was hampered by severe mystifications and disfigurements, since both Constantine and Charlemagne took over the office of "protector." As a result of the symbiosis with the secular power, the consciousness of "lordship" came more and more to the fore. In the ninth and tenth centuries the apostolic office became a football of feudalism; in the twelfth to fourteenth centuries it became an almost totalitarian power; and in the fourteenth and fifteenth centuries it became a chaos through the Western Schism. It was shaken by the Reformation in the sixteenth and seventeenth centuries and then caught up in renewals and litigations until Vatican I and post-Vatican discussions over the relationship of the primate to the episcopate under the aegis of curial centralism. So far as the valuation of the papacy was concerned, the Reformation was a revolution which sought refuge from a desperate situation in German corporate law. According to the characterization made by a Lutheran ecclesiastical jurist, what remained were "functional sees without orders (ordo)." Instead of the intended union with the ancient church, there was a union with the authority of the provincial princes, and instead of the spiritual fatherhood and sonship between Paul and Timothy, between the consecrator and the consecrated, the creed took on an entirely new educative meaning, detached from the personal tradition. The biblical way is the personal transmission of the responsible service of the shepherd. God has taken men into His service. The Lord says to His apostles: "He who hears you, hears Me." Paul writes to Timothy: "Protect the good entrusted to you by the Holy Spirit and give it to the keeping of men you can trust who are assigned the task of teaching it to others." The Lutheran theologian H. Asmussen says, "Under this aspect the position of the reformers does not attain the truth of the ancient biblical church because it dissolves the position of bearer of ecclesiastical authority." They believed that there was a succession of credos and that this alone sufficed for succession.

Let us turn to what is truly worth considering in the recent history of Protestant theology; something visible in the few passages quoted above. Thanks to intensified biblical studies (Kittel-

Friedrich's theological dictionary forms a testimony which has no counterpart on the Catholic side); thanks to the fraternal meetings of Protestant theologians with Anglican and Eastern Orthodox colleagues in the World Council of Churches and with their Catholic colleagues in *Una Sancta*, a mellowing of the old lines of opposition concerning apostolic succession has begun which promises to be of the greatest significance for further developments. A few examples: L. Newbigin, bishop of the Church of South India, writes in *The Household of God* that as far as the "Catholic" wing of the *Oekumene* is concerned, the bishop's authority belongs to the very essence of the church and as far as the Protestant wing is concerned, it is of "high worth." This concession rests on Protestant premises. Nevertheless, it is recognized that reunification is a command of the Lord, and that the apostolic tradition of the East-West Church has *more* weight than the separation in the sixteenth century, understandable in the situation, but unendurable permanently. A Lutheran like Edmund Schlink finds apostolic succession desirable, Ethelbert Stauffer sees that the succession to the office of bishop is within the framework of the Gospel, and Werner Elert asserts that the liturgical and sacramental celebrations presuppose the supervision of the episcopate. Even the reform theologian, J. J. von Allmen, professes that apostolic succession is the very essence of the ordering principle proper to the Church. In his introduction to the French edition of Gregory Dix's significant work, *Le ministère dans l'Église* (1955), he writes: "The full valuation of the office of pastor is the first ecumenical problem. To evade it is to evade union itself. Corresponding to the threefold office of Christ as Preacher, Priest and Pastor, the life of the Church is based on faith, the administration of the sacraments and the direction of the flock. To deny this would be to deprive the Lord of part of His Body." The validity of the consecration to authority is put in question if the apostolic succession is denied. With the same intention, the representatives of Ecumenical Catholicity have set for themselves the goal of becoming theologically acclimatized to thoughts of a return to an apostolic order native both to the Bible and the ancient church. They have "a new consciousness of the powers which have been given to the spiritual authority," says H. D. Wendland. "It has cost the Protestant church unspeakable effort to this very day to free itself from perverting contradictions, and to recognize the mixture of spiritual inequality with spiritual equality to which the Church of the apostles testifies in the writings of the New Testament." According to H. Asmussen, "It remains a serious question whether the orders given from dire necessity in the Reformation have ever emerged from the stage of provisionality. . . . One cannot raise 'dire need' to the level of a principle. Once more it must be asked how succession in the Church is to be viewed in its earthly definition. . . . The authority of directing the Church cannot be self-established; neither can it be established by official actions. Ordination is a pneumatic power, the point at which the *pneuma* affects the succession. Consequently the power of ordination can be imparted only in a sacred service."

Naturally a few questions still require clarification. An ever recurring concern of our Protestant brothers is the apparent formalism of the line of succession, the automatic mechanism of succession to office. What Karl Barth writes in his *Church Dogmatics* is highly interesting: "The idea of succession in the ancient church could be justified (as the knowledge of the co-dwelling of Christ and the Church), and in respect to the 'thatness' of it, no objections can be made; objections can be made only to the 'how' of it — and even in this respect no fundamental objection on our side can be raised against the conception of the 'apostolate in Peter,' nor against the possibility of a primate in the Church. Protest is raised only against the contention that the highest power (from the apostles and from the first Peter) proceeded automatically to each succeeding Roman bishop, as if the succession could be viewed as other than pneumatic or, to put it more precisely, as though the pneumatic could be reduced to the secular actuality of a list of bishops."

The objection to the mechanism of succession, it appears to us, deals basically with the administration of the sacraments, and is based on the misunderstanding that according to Catholic doctrine, the *opus operatum,* the outer thing or act, is efficacious in itself alone. In truth, considered in themselves, the consecration to office, baptism, the consecration of the bread and wine and the forgiveness of sins, are not efficacious without faith on the human side as a disposition for the consecration by the Holy Spirit. Thus men are simply, as St. Augustine explains, instruments for the invisible gift. Consequently, although the higher powers are in a spatio-temporal dimension, since it is a man who is doing the ordaining (baptizing, consecrating, forgiving, etc.), nevertheless their basis is not so much the holiness of the human framework, or the historically-determined line of succession of the act of consecration back to the time of the apostles, as it is the operation of the Holy Spirit Who transcends both time and space. Even though severe spiritual abuses occurred in the feudal society of former centuries, even though illicitly-consecrated individuals were forced into the Church by the secular power, even though Popes (justly or unjustly) were deposed — no theologian maintains that the original link has been cut off by men, and that the continuity of the grace-giving Spirit has been broken. Although Donatists and others made the "holiness" of the person concerned the condition for valid consecration, it is interesting to notice that the Augsburg Confession kept aloof from this view, since "the sacraments and the Word are made efficacious through the appointment of Christ even when they are handled by evil persons." As far as lists of bishops are concerned, they are no more to ecclesiastical life than a family history is for the life of a family.

The position of the Protestants, however, goes deeper and should be taken seriously by us. Stählin says: "Certainly the unity of the Church is enclosed in its historical continuity, and this continuity on the horizontal level is subordinated on the vertical level to the operations of the supernatural First Cause. What is questionable is the self-assurance in the administration of the deposit of grace, the impression of having Christ's presence at one's disposal. Is any promise given unconditionally, is it not always bound to obedience to the word and spirit of Christ?" This is the serious worry that moves sincere friends of ecumenism like Peter Brunner or Ernst Kinder. "The traditions in the Church," says Kinder, "have a tendency to absolutize themselves and to emancipate themselves from their functional relationship to the Bible . . . as though they had an exclusive lease on God's saving powers." Our response is: Never will there be a perfect guarantee against the abuse of what is holy. The teachings of Holy Scripture and the history of the Church are very clear on what attitudes can be taken to avoid severe failures and scandals: there is always the free word of the prophets and obligatory fraternal admonishments (involving at times the admonishment of a superior in rank by an inferior) and in extreme cases the holy right and duty of opposition to the scandals of a superior. Thomas Aquinas praises Paul for his opposition to the dangerous position of the first apostle concerning the sharing of meals between Jewish and gentile converts. Can a consecrated person then be spoken of as having the deposit of grace at his disposal? Foolish and misleading words can provide the occasion for such an interpretation — I myself have heard some. The doctrines of faith, however, should not be measured by the inaccuracies of a preacher or the lightly considered formulations of a journalist. I think that Protestant theologians do not doubt the objectively given power of a spiritual authority. The power "to bind and to loose," is promised and given by God; otherwise all talk about responsible services by the Church would be senseless. This is not to say, however, that man can dispose of this divine gift according to caprice. This authority must be understood in the spirit of Christ, in the spirit of love. It would be sinful for man to act high-handedly and the saying that "all sin avenges itself on earth" holds equally for the Church.

It is well said by Karl Rahner: "The promise that the gates of hell will never prevail against the Church does not mean the promise of a strength and safety that is always tangible for us; it is, rather, the promise of the power, which is God's alone, on behalf of the weak and constantly threatened men who form the Church. The men in the Church may well feel assured that 'nothing can really happen to the Church' because time and again nothing has happened to the Church which is in God's hands despite the men who lazily or fearfully (we add — arrogantly) have abandoned Her."

Now it appears that Rahner himself raises a question in another article when he places the spiritual power in an easily misleading proximity with an unconditional "disposability," and just at the point where the powers of the Church are concentrated in the Papacy. He first says what is evident: "Only a totalitarian, not a Pope, could regard the free charisma in the Church through the action of the Holy Spirit as a diminution, or a danger to perennial authority; and this is valid especially when a charismatic bishop, in the name of Christ, leads to pasture the flock which Christ has entrusted to him." Later on, in respect to the full powers of the Pope, he says: "To a certain extent, the proper limitation — that is, a limitation factually proportioned (i.e., through positive human ecclesiastical law) — to the events and to the time of the spiritual situation is something that cannot be constitutionally regulated by strict material norms. There is no tangible evidence to show that the factual relation between the episcopate and the primate in the ecclesiastical jurisdiction of competency is correct and suitable. Only the governance of the Holy Spirit can see to it that this competition in practice . . . takes place in such a way that it works for what is best for the Church. When the relationship between the two powers is properly considered, there is no norm which precludes a Pope in practice from taking all power to himself in such a way that actually only the name of divine power remains for a bishop . . . for no earthly tests of an authoritative kind overrule the judgments of the Holy See; the highest competency belongs to the Pope and it does not give and cannot give a particular and ultimate right of opposition that the Church can concretely maintain. (Furthermore it is a right that the Church should not give because of the presence of the Holy Spirit promised to it.)" In a theological discussion Rahner clarified his view in the following way: "From the promise of the Spirit, we can infer that if a future Peter XX *de facto* wanted to transgress his spiritual authority in a serious matter, at that very moment he would suddenly die."

One can only be grateful that the question has been made so clear in respect to this crucial point. As our basic thought let us keep in mind the principle expressed in the following words of M. Pribilla: "The Spirit allows a good deal of room to human freedom. Christ, the wellspring, is never dry, but we men participate in His blessings only insofar as we make ourselves receptive to them. In this connection between divine and human factors it is basic that both the growth and decline of Christendom depend on human factors." Dietrich Bonhoeffer expresses it this way: "I do not believe that God is a timeless Fate; rather I believe that He awaits and answers sincere prayers and responsible actions." And H. Dombois: "Indeed all earthly tendencies have not killed the Church. What the Holy Spirit does through the epochs in the history of the Church, and what human effort achieves in obedience to faith are evidently incomparable; on the other hand it is equally clear that the protection and reawakening of the Church is not accomplished without our human effort. No guarantee can chain up the Holy Spirit, but we are asked to take in all seriousness the divine service, teaching and order." The question is: Does the Spirit act, in the case of transgressions of spiritual authority (as with Boniface VIII), as a sort of *Deus ex Machina,* or does God wish to utilize the pneumatic powers within the Church as a corrective against a threatening absolutism? Since the authority of the bishop is based on no less a divine apostolic basis than the authority of Peter, does it not require some type of ecclesiastical judicial prerogative in order that it may fulfill its mission with full decisiveness? Is there not in the inspired New Testament a *de facto* approval of the opposition of the last apostle to a dangerous measure by the first apostle? Do the bishops only represent the Pope, and not rather the "college of apostles"? Has this (the college of bishops) its power from the Pope, or rather from Christ? And does not the Church stand by the power of divine law which, antecedent to Church law, is based solely on the "apostles" and on "the prophets"? Jesus prayed for Peter that he should strengthen the brethren, and when he refused in Antioch, Brother Paul knew himself called by the Spirit to give his admonition with full apostolic power. If, in the hypothetical case presented by Rahner, the bishops feel themselves bound in duty to act, would a Pope then be valid as the bearer of the Holy Spirit who wished to oppose both the episcopate and the people of the Church, and thus place the Church in a position where there was nothing left but to await a miracle?

I confess myself deeply impressed by the confident assurance of Rahner's statement that the direction of the Church by the Holy Spirit is ultimately not an affair of human guarantees and the assurances of ecclesiastical law, but that it derives from a divine promise. We are in accord on this. What it seems important to me to emphasize is the means, closely associated to faith, in which the divine Spirit actualizes His promise in history through human instruments, and how a refusal of co-responsibility toward God's counsel brings about sickness for the members of the historical Church.

On the historical plane the Spirit's promise of God's fidelity is actually not effective independent of devotion to the faith by those elected to it and responsible for it; it is, rather, conditioned by their faithfulness to the Spirit of Christ. We are fundamentally in accord with the representatives of Ecumenical Catholicity on this decisive question which they have placed before us. Only, perhaps, we do not consider it as seriously as it should be considered. Certainly Paul says in his Epistle to the Romans that the promises of the spirit cannot be simply annulled by human infidelity, but they can be limited by a "holy delay" for a while (for a thousand years, which are only a day in the sight of God). What a darkening of the saving mission of the Church was indicated by the pretensions of the medieval hierarchy, especially when they were cloaked with an appeal to sacred scripture! And does the neglect of the eucharistic service through the centuries mean anything other than a shocking loss of religious substance for the spiritual nourishment of the flock of Christ, a loss of substance that weighed not only on the flock but on the shepherds themselves, because people permitted themselves all too easily to be satisfied with an unconditional promise! Did not the Reformation itself occur because the co-responsibility of the episcopate for the conduct of the Roman curia in serious matters was no longer taken seriously? And in regard to the split itself, Newman wrote (to be sure as an Anglican, but later on even more professedly as a Catholic) these serious lines:

> If we have anything to learn from the history of Judaism, it is not improbable that the Christian Church has forfeited a portion of the promises; but we shall find, I think, in the New Testament that the promises made to her actually did depend in part upon a condition which now for many centuries she (as the totality of those validly baptized) has broken. This condition is Unity, which Christ and his Apostles made to some extent the sacramental channel through which all the gifts of the Spirit, and among them purity of doctrine, were secured to the Church.

We must regard these considerations, based on the historical predicament of the Church, even more closely and speak concretely in order to avoid vagueness. Let us assume that our Catholic co-responsibility for the split, brought about by mutual fault of our fathers and perpetuated by ourselves, was taken seriously not only by theologians and active lay groups, but also by the bishops, especially the bishops (not unimportant for the collective Church) of the confessionally mixed countries. And let us further assume that while looking toward a papal definition, we faced the question whether we and the pastors of the Church, in the presence of the guilt-laden predicament of Christianity, must not concern ourselves, before everything else, with the unity of the divided Christian community. The question involves the Church as a whole, especially the bishops, and not only the see of Peter, which according to the express declaration of Vatican I must be asked if it has a final decision. Now I think that the question is not once and for all a clear-cut theological question; rather I think it presupposes an ethico-religious "pre-decision,"

whether the people of the Church and its responsible pastors want
to meditate on concrete historical actualities, on the broken existence of the Christian community in the world. For the sake of
Christ, in responsibility for the Kingdom of God, and for the moral
worth of the Christian faith in the West and in its missions, such
considerations must lead to the recognition that nothing more
important can happen for the Church as a whole. For Roman
Catholic Christianity, the Council of Trent has striven for the unity
that was possible in its historical time; it limited itself theologically
to the most necessary current clarification of the controversial
questions and consciously abstained from a dogmatic completion
by its own power. Gradually the broad groups composing the
Church's people hardly thought of their responsibility to Christendom as a whole; rarely did they think of the necessity for
amendment (amendment seemed necessary only for personal sins).
If the Church in itself is spoken of as a kind of abstract idea, then
it is the one true Church insofar as it unites in itself all the essential
marks and characteristics, and insofar as it conducts itself with the
fullness of all its powers. This is theologically incontestable. But
can one neglect the historically empirical reality which is revealed
by the separate growth of a "conservative Catholic" and a "reform
Catholic" wing of Christendom, the one with a culpable retardation
of readiness for reform, the other culpable of "revolutionizing"
the reform, yet neither of them finally wanting separation even
though they are compelled to separate politically? Can one convinced of the correct idea of the Church's completeness and
integrity in its very essence, then act as if the Church did not
live at all in history, and as if "the completed Church" could forego
its moral co-responsibility for the split, and its religious duty to
heal this split, before it does anything else? The question is not
theological; the theological truth of dogmatic propositions is not
under discussion. Neither is it an opportunity to dogmatize; more
widely and relevantly than the secular word "opportunity" permits
us to suppose, it deals with an ethico-religious responsibility.
Should we in this culpable existence of historical division take up
the spirit of Jesus Christ as a self-evident privilege for our own

special ecclesiastical development? Can we do this while we evade the moral "pre-decision," or have forgotten it in becoming accustomed to the situation? It is historically understandable that at the moment this type of question lies far from the sight of such church circles as those, for instance, in South America, who, without giving serious thought to their ecclesiastical existence in Christ, and the most pressing missionary tasks within their own countries, prefer to specialize even further their Marian cult. "How very much exaggerations of a falsely understood Mariology can deteriorate genuine Catholic thought," a leading Catholic theologian wrote me in this regard.

The Papacy within the circle of the apostles and the continuity of this structure is nearly as well attested in Scripture and the ancient Church as is the Church itself. The basic proofs for Catholicism have impressed many Protestants. Also the advertence of K. Hofstetter and others to early Christian witnesses of the replacement of Jerusalem by Rome as the Mother-Church and the chief location of the total Church are being justly noticed. But the authority of Peter in the ancient Church cannot be easily compared with our present papal authority, and Catholic theologians such as B. Bootmann, P. Benoit, O. Rousseau and the friends of the highly respected P. Couturier cannot help but admit this. Developments understood pneumatically but not organically are grounded in the very historical existence of the Church; but so few developments in the Faith and ecclesiastical life can be fundamentally thrown into question that we shall have to measure these and any other results coming from them by the standard of Scripture, by the prototype of the ancient Church, and by the overall spirit exhibited by them. The gradations of responsibilities, the relationship of the apostolate to the testimonial of the Spirit, of the episcopate to the primate, is essential for the Church. Autocratic tendencies are temptations and are thus not in the spirit of Christ. "No single one can want to be all; only all can be all, and the unity that of a totality," says Moehler in a classic phrase. Believing that he was making the essence and greatness of the Church more familiar to Field-Marshal Montgomery, the English convert

Arnold Lunn said: "You see, the Catholic Church is like the Eighth Army; it has its discipline and its leaders." He may have considered such an image modern and purposeful — but measured by the apostolic Church it gives a distorted image of the authority and mystery of the Church. If such images were to become more widespread, we should be very grateful for an inhibiting ecumenical partnership.

The significance of ecumenical partnership for the development of modern theology and the care of souls cannot be hidden from anyone in our day. Many evangelical theologians give us an example of their love of unity by re-examining their own position. We should not expect everything from them without laying some bricks of our own on the road to reunification. I say "we," not only "the Roman Catholics" or the Pope, for on the deepest level we are united in guilt and grace. Being ready to heal the broken unity of Christians in accord with Christ's serious command is identical with reflection and atonement for all those taking part in it.

The first thing that honest ecumenical amendment involves is the acknowledgment that our separated fellow Christians are brothers in Christ, thanks to the grace of God and Holy Baptism, the power of God's Word in them, and finally to the presence and activity of the Holy Spirit in their midst; acknowledgment of their love (given by faith) of Holy Scripture and especially acknowledgment of the truly Christian life, not of all, but of many in their love of God and neighbor with their whole hearts; acknowledgment of their efforts toward unity, not always as one might think solely with Protestants, but also in fraternal dialogue with the Catholic communities that have joined the dialogue. All this we know from experience and we testify to it with great joy. Our best theologians and spiritual directors have Protestant friends who have no desire to lure them from their position or from their work for the Kingdom of God.

Secondly, in regard to ecumenical reflection, there is the need to become prepared to learn from each other in mutual helpfulness for the Kingdom of God. The Council of Trent adopted many of the Protestant options of its time; present-day theologians learn much from Karl Barth, O. Cullmann and other Protestant exegetes. It would certainly not be detracting from Catholic truth to point out that the realization of certain values in the life of the Church came into being only as a result of the encounter with our Protestant fellow-Christians. The justification of sinful man through God's grace is not closely connected in the Protestant realm with the sacramental life; on the other hand it might be said that the belief in justification as good Protestants experience it, cut free from the battle against "works," has nothing un-Catholic about it. Rather it discloses a personal immediacy to God which brings great simplicity and purposeful direction toward what is truly necessary — a simplicity and purposeful direction that cannot be replaced by theological knowledge or through many devotions. After getting over the first surprise it was a great joy to me when Rudolph Otto answered my query as to what was essentially Protestant in this way: "Justification by faith." I then said to him: "If this is truly the decisive point, then many of us are good Protestants and many of you are good Catholics." St. Thomas Aquinas teaches: "Not on the moral (the fulfillment of the law) does the confidence in justification lie, but in faith alone. We believe that man is justified (participates as a child of God) by faith without performing works of the Law." In this regard Lyonnet observes: "With St. Paul what is contrasted is all moral activity on one side and faith (in the grace of God) on the other," and according to an explanation given by H. Küng that means: "The confident yielding of the self to God's grace as a response to God's action."

Another thing that we can learn is the Protestant valuation of Holy Scripture as the normative basis of revelation and piety. We could certainly learn this theology from the Church Fathers and from the example of many saints such as the little St. Theresa; our discourse however with our contemporaries means — thanks to the questions they put to us — a wholesome needling. Biblical studies play a somewhat modest role in the present-day education of our theologians, and this is also true — prescinding from the Biblical

Institute — for Roman institutions as well. In the homes of Protestant pastors I found a custom which says far more than many discussions: in the morning before breakfast the father of the house reads a short excerpt from Holy Scripture and then a daily excerpt of the Roman Mass from the missal as an inspiration for the labors of the day. I could think of nothing more beautiful for Catholic homes since only a few can initiate the day's work with Holy Mass.

The following example should show that our Protestant fellow-Christians can teach us much about the Christocentric applications of our theology and piety which is truly Catholic, but which at times is not too clearly discernable. The English Catholic journalist Michel de la Bedoyere writes from his life and observations that his religious instruction within his circle had been heavily loaded with catechetical concepts, moral definitions, and rules for devotions and asceticism. It had also been characterized for many others by a strange hunger for prophecies, the visions of children, stigmata, etc. And so he spent decades missing the forest for the trees until he discovered how great and simple Christ's message is, since it reveals to us what God is to men and that we, in Christ, are the New Man. It is sad that Protestants have lost the meaning of the veneration of saints and above all of the Holy Mother of God; but to a large extent this is a reaction to an overemphasis in practice on the part of Catholics — an overemphasis which, in those countries barely touched by biblical instructions, has tended to a certain displacement of the Christocentric character of Catholicism.

From the foregoing it would follow that the increasing proximity of many Protestant theologians to Catholic truths which had previously been lost should be answered on our side by "not only a sympathetic, but also by a concrete search for what is valid in the reform positions." Varying Congar's inferences, Karl Rahner writes in his essay "On Conversion" that besides tendencies toward dissolution in contemporary Protestantism, there is not only much genuine Christian substance to be observed, but also "in a long history outside the Catholic Church, genuinely Christian possibilities were actualized in theology, piety, the liturgy, the communal life and art . . . which have not been realized by us in the Catholic Church, although in themselves they belong to the actual fullness of the historical development of that which is Christian." How much is lacking to us in Catholic Christianity because — for fear of the "Protestant spirit" — we fettered the genuine evangelical freedom of witness and self-responsibility in the realm of the spiritual life as it had not been fettered in the Patristic or the Medieval period! How Newman suffered over this! On the other hand what heavy losses and splinterings has protestantism suffered and continues to suffer because she — to name the most decisive factor — let fall the authority of the apostolic office as the antithesis of the free testimony of the Spirit. The post-Reformation generations have been hindered in their receptivity to many Catholic truths; but they sincerely want to hold themselves to Christ's revelation, and, thus, in a formal sense, they are not heretics. Rather they are much more bound to Christ's Church by their membership in Him. This can be said in another way: "They are our fellow Christians and in all truth our comrades in faith with whom we know ourselves bound in the great decision which is posed to modern men everywhere: the choice between belief and disbelief" (W. H. van de Pol).

Do ecumenical endeavors have any prospects of success? There cannot be a union with Protestantism for the simple reason that there is no such thing as "Protestantism." There are only Protestantisms. And at the present the members of the Protestant Church hardly permit themselves to think of a deeper movement toward Catholic unity. Temporarily there are theological and religious inner circles who are in close prayerful and dialectical community with their Catholic brothers. But then the Catholic Church itself is not presently ready for a larger ecumenical movement. Newman's words: "It must now prepare itself just for converts," apply to an even greater extent to the difficult preparation of the whole Church in regard to the responsibility for reunification through serious reflection or "repentance" (to use Bishop M. Besson's word). Nevertheless with God nothing is impossible. According to the testimony of those very close to him, Pius XI faced this problem seriously as a part of his purpose to renew all things in Christ. He was very much concerned as to how he could effect a reversal necessary for the sake of Christian unity, from the high point of hierarchical centralism to the synthesis of love of the Church Fathers, and ultimately according to the original apostolic image. Humanly speaking, it is not probable that we shall realize such possibilities tomorrow or the day after, and thus approach Unity with the great Protestant bodies. Nevertheless this is the decision before which Christianity stands. But the majority does yet not understand how dangerous a refusal would be. The greatest dangers, says Karl Rahner, are those one does not notice and the most dangerous decision is the decision not to decide.

Is it too bold to hope and to strive for repentance in the ecumenical sphere? A counter-question: Is it not cowardly, and a sign of little faith not to hope and strive? Faith is a pledge for the human inability to see God. "Faith involves the courage to make a wager" (J. H. Newman). Faith in the meaning of Jesus is a surrender to the Kingdom of God that is always coming into time. Have not all the heroes of faith died without having experienced the fulfillment of the promise? If this is the case — and the Bible proclaims it — then slogans like "Utopia" have no justification. It would amount to saying that the apostolic Church itself is one of the never-to-be-discovered Utopias of history. We would then be refusing to adopt the apostolic ideal of the Church as the mirror by which to test our historical reality. This amounts to subjecting divine law, and the duty to be faithful to the structure of the apostolic Church, to our own special claims. In this way we are telling Jesus Christ (sorrowfully to be sure, but in fact) that His Testament does not interest us and that we prefer to remain divided — since there is no way to Unity. We would rather sing our own text in the theological war than sing Christ's praise. The first choir proclaims: "We Protestant Christians perpetuate the emergency methods of Luther and Calvin in order to keep out of the Pope's snare." The second choir: "We Catholics perpetuate the summit of the development which led us from the 'Collegial-Petrine Church' to the 'Centralized-Petrine Church.'"

But perhaps we will probe ourselves seriously to discover whether Christ's call for reflection at the beginning of His mission, and His prayer for unity as His last testimonial, can be as existential a question for us as it once was for the people of the promise.

PIET FRANSEN, S.J.

EPISCOPAL CONFERENCES: CRUCIAL PROBLEM OF THE COUNCIL*

ONE of the central, crucial questions under discussion at the Second Vatican Council is that concerning the role of the world-wide episcopacy within the Church. There is, moveover, a danger that declarations of principle on the nature of episcopal power would remain ineffective if matters are left on an abstract level. We are not speaking of the difficulty of a similar dogmatic formulation, since this does not yet seem well prepared. The Church is not primarily a system of dogma, but a living organism. To the degree that this episcopal power will begin to have concrete application in the life of the Church, we can expect lasting results. There is the same necessity in connection with another urgent question, the role of laymen. If the Council does not succeed in laying down the primary ecclesiastical structures permitting laymen to take their share of responsibility in the life of the Church, it must be feared that declarations of principle will have no aftermath. According to the statements of several bishops coming from Rome after their work on one of the commissions, theoretical problems in regard to these two vital questions are seen as particularly difficult.

Contemporary Origin and Later Evolution

The custom of episcopal conferences gradually established itself in the Church after the French Revolution and Napoleon. Three distinct periods can be distinguished.

* Reprinted with permission from Cross Currents, Summer, 1963. (Translated by Joseph E. Cunneen.)

Preliminary attempts were made during the second half of the nineteenth century. The Church had been extremely weakened by the Revolution and the Napoleonic wars, and was attacked on all sides. It was the period of the Kulturkampf, freemasonry, and an aggressively triumphant bourgeois liberalism. The bishops of the *Ancien Régime* were part of the state administration. Under Napoleon a single council was called by Napoleon himself; all other reunions of bishops were forbidden. He was so suspicious of the episcopacy that the bishops could not even come to Paris without his permission, and even when they were called in by his minister Portal, it was always separately.

In the rare studies of this subject, one forgets to mention the example of the Belgian Church, which played the role of pilot-Church after the revolution of 1830. Gregory XVI had declared that the Belgian revolution had abolished the Concordats with Belgium of 1801 and 1827. In addition, the Belgian constitution had accepted separation between Church and State, a new formula regarded with considerable suspicion by Metternich, the alliance, and the Roman Curia. After 1830 the Belgian bishops adopted the practice of assembling once a year in a palace of the arch-bishop of Malines. In 1837 Msgr. Capaccini, pro-secretary of State at the Vatican, praised "the happy union which marks the Belgian episcopacy." This was also the opinion of the nuncio Pecci during his brief stay at Brussels. The biographer of Cardinal Sterckx, A. Simon, writes in this connection, "He understood the meaning of our liberties." It is likely that the future Leo XIII learned to understand at Brussels the advantages of this new freedom of the Church in the State.

Rome nevertheless insisted that the Belgian bishops should be united in a regional council. The primate of Belgium always preferred the more discreet formula of an episcopal conference, not wanting to arouse the aggressive tendencies of a government that was jealous of its authority and its freedom. "Decisions were taken unanimously; if one of the bishops did not share the opinion of his colleagues, the matter was left open." At the request of Rome, papal nuncios were invited after a few years. From the beginning, however, the Belgian bishops were determined to assume their full pastoral responsibilities in the territories confided to their care, a tradition they had continued to maintain.

After the revolution of 1848, the movement spread in Europe. The German bishops met for the first time in Wurzburg in 1848. Since 1869 they had been meeting at Fulda, and since 1850 the bishops of Bavaria have gathered at Freising — with the approval of Pius IX in 1864. Austrian bishops met at Vienna, beginning in 1848, with government approval and support. There were regional conferences in Italy, especially in Umbria, from 1848, while the Irish bishops met for the first time in Dublin in 1854.

Leo XIII, perhaps because of his experiences in Belgium, strongly encouraged these regular consultations of the national bishops. On December 8, 1882, and May 5, 1902, he recommended it to the Spanish bishops, and on September 14, 1886, and June 25, 1891 to the Portuguese. Similar encouragement was given to the Austrian bishops (March 3, 1891), to the Hungarians (September 2, 1893), and the Brazilians (July 2, 1894). Under his influence the Congregation of Propaganda proposed detailed instructions for the calling of synods in China and India. Under his protection the Armenians in 1890 and the Greek-Melkite uniates in 1900 restored a custom which was always more widespread in the East.

It appeared that these conferences would more and more come to replace the former national synods. Nevertheless, according to the intentions of the Pope one of the purposes of episcopal conferences was still to prepare the work of regional and national councils, which according to ancient law alone possessed the competence to legislate in those matters which concerned the local Church. In several countries, especially younger countries like the United States and Australia, such synods laid the foundations for an organization and a diocesan legislation adapted to the new conditions of these faraway continents. The important national council of Baltimore in 1884 was prepared at Rome, and the first Latin American council was celebrated at Rome under Leo's pontificate in 1900.

The Pope frequently insisted on the importance of regular meetings. He reminded the bishops of the example of the Church's enemies, who gathered outside its frontiers, or the example of laymen in various countries who met to discuss political and religious problems. Under his pontificate the Congregation of Bishops and Regulars developed its first statutes — in 1898 for Austria, and a first outline of canonical structure in 1900 for Latin America. A circular from the same Congregation (August 24, 1869) sanctioned this custom.

After the death of Leo, one was under the impression that this movement slowed down. From 1906 to 1907 the Assembly of the Bishops of France met three times to reorganize the Church after the law of separation of December 9, 1905. It seemed that the bishops were satisfied after that to address themselves to the Roman Curia to resolve their problems. In any case, the Code of Canon Law published in 1917 contained a whole chapter on the organization of plenary and provincial councils (Bk. II, t.t. VII, ch. vii), with only one canon at the end dealing with episcopal conferences in the same ecclesiastical province. "Unless the Holy See has decided otherwise for specific regions, the metropolitan, or in his absence, the oldest bishop among the suffragans in terms of the norms of canon 184, should call together the ordinaries at least every five years, at a date determined by the metropolitan or one of the bishops belonging to the same ecclesiastical province, in order to deliberate together and to see what measures should be adopted to promote the good of religion in their dioceses and prepare the question they will wish to treat in a future provincial council" (canon 292, § 1).

It is immediately noticeable that according to canon law today these episcopal conferences do not possess any legislative power. They are essentially consultative reunions. Only a plenary or provincial council — the latter should be called every twenty years (canon 283) — have the power to formulate decrees, which can only be promulgated after the approbation of the Sacred Congregation of the Council (canon 291, § 1). They acquire the force of law over the whole territory of a province or of several ecclesiastical provinces from this fact (canon 291, § 2). An ecclesiastical province, we recall, is composed of several dioceses, dependent on a single metropolitan. A plenary council, according to canon law, is a regional conciliar reunion which brings together several ecclesiastical provinces (canon 281).

Another aspect of the Code places episcopal conferences under the jurisdiction of the Sacred Congregation of the Council, with the exception of territories dependent on the Congregation of Propaganda (canon 250, § 4).

This first period of episcopal conferences is extremely interesting, and Plöchl is right to ask for a history of their evolution. Such an account would have to go back even before the French Revolution, as Lalmant suggests in the *Dictionaire du Droit Canonique*.

Understandably, this evolution met with opposition. Plöchl mentions the suspicion of the Roman Curia with its instinctive fears of the conciliar or anti-papal influence of Gallicanism or Febronianism. Austria represents the leading example of this danger, because of governmental influence. It was the Austrian practice and experience which inspired the instruction of the Congregation of Bishops and Priests-Regular under Leo XIII. Nevertheless, the suspicion of the Curia seems to have been less strong then than in our own time. In the instruction of the Congregation of Bishops and Priests-Regular (June 22, 1898, no. 6), it is explicitly mentioned that the conclusions of these assemblies are not subject to revision by the Holy See. One of the probable motives for this seems to be that in the eyes of Rome these conferences did not have the ability to legislate. In any case, after the Code of Canon Law was revised (1917), the Congregation frequently reminded the bishops that episcopal conferences remained under its jurisdiction.

Nevertheless, during the nineteenth century the bishops were faced with another source of difficulty which happily no longer exists. In several European countries every reunion of bishops had to be submitted to the prior approval of the government.

There is another interesting detail. Especially in Austria, episcopal conferences allowed for the participation of priests and sometimes even of laymen. This practice also disappeared with the

Code, perhaps even before it. In his letter to Cardinal Gibbons (January 22, 1899), Leo XIII condemned that aspect of "Americanism" which demanded a greater freedom of action for laymen as in accordance with the democratic custom of the country. We cannot understand today the attitudes of some American bishops when they hear discussions of the responsibility of laymen in the life of the Church if we forget that there was a case of the Archbishop of New York being expelled from his episcopal residence on Fifth Avenue by laymen, who under the law were considered the owners of the property. A serious history of "trusteeism" is still to be written. It would help to explain a situation which today astonishes us and often gives rise to irritation.

Let us go on to the second period. We can be more brief, because it is better known, including the years just after the First World War, and especially after the Second. The code had sketched out a beginning of a canonical structure and had made episcopal conferences obligatory for the whole Church.

Meanwhile the Church had liberated itself in most countries from the tutelage of the state, which no longer thought of interfering in the internal affairs of the Church. Means of communication had brought men closer together. Modern technics facilitated the organization of many kinds of meetings. The parliamentary spirit encouraged bishops to profit from modern experiences by holding discussion and consultation, first on the national level, and soon on the international level. The bishops were compelled to follow the movement developing within the Church by which large religious organizations, like Catholic Action, tended to become national, and by this fact cut across diocesan boundaries, and in large countries even included more than one ecclesiastical province. These groups look to single directives which would include their national field of action, and have no desire to be limited by multiple diocesan particularisms. Serious crises were shaking our whole western civilization without sparing the Church, which had to look for solutions to problems on the national level. This appeared more and more obvious in regard to social questions, the problems connected with Catholic schools, and the political issues which divide a whole country. The world is rapidly being united. It must be said that in a number of countries the hierarchy seems to have lagged behind in this movement toward unity that proceeds outside its ranks and even among the faithful.

During this period, episcopal conferences were established in several countries, their statutes previously approved by the Sacred Congregation of the Council. We would like to present two typical examples, that of France, and that of South America.

The Assembly of Cardinals and Archbishops (ACA) of France was founded in 1919. From the beginning it organized itself and established working commissions — including those for Catholic Action and education — and a general commission. After World War II, the first plenary assembly of the French episcopacy took place (June 3–4, 1951), after having been approved by Pius XII in his letter to Cardinal Lienart (May 26, 1947). Since 1951 this episcopal assembly has created fifteen episcopal commissions, made up of bishops mandated by their colleagues to deal with a specific sector of pastoral work and the apostolate. These two assemblies now have their own permanent secretariat and press service.

These assemblies do not have any legislative or synodal power. But their decisions can, naturally, enter into canon law to the extent that the bishops wish to promulgate them in their respective dioceses. This remark holds true for all episcopal conferences established in accordance with actual law today. Their moral authority, however, is very high. It is impossible to understand the history of the Church of France from 1951 on without taking into consideration this living unity of the national episcopacy. One need only recall the influence of various Directories published under its auspices, which are consulted even in other countries. During this period France experienced terrible crises — the war in Indochina, the war in Algeria which threatened to become a civil war, and several grave political and social crises which almost split the country. It should be recalled that in the nineteenth century these same national crises gave rise to deep divisions among Christians, and even among bishops. The Church of France has emerged from all these trials strengthened and with greater unity. This unity of the episcopacy has allowed it to accept its responsibilities before the state with complete independence. It has even been said that some non-Catholics have come to favor a concordat between Church and State, because this agreement between the Holy See and the state would better serve the purpose of tying the Church to the existing power.

There is another episcopal conference which has become famous in a very brief time, CELAM, the Latin American episcopal council. The plenary council of Latin American bishops, held in Rome in 1900 at the invitation of Leo XIII, had no successor. In 1955 on the occasion of the International Eucharistic Congress of Rio de Janeiro, Pius XII called for an episcopal conference of all Latin America under the presidency of Cardinal Piazza. The conference formulated a common declaration and various conclusions. Its principal act was the creation of CELAM, with a permanent secretariat in Bogota publishing its own bulletin. This council represents the national episcopal conferences, all of which send their representative. There is a president and two vice-presidents, chosen by the over-all membership for a two-year period.

It is important to take into account the motives which led to the establishment of CELAM. They are summuned up in article 97, chapter XI of the conclusions of the 1955 Rio conference:

"The general conference of the Latin-American episcopacy has unanimously approved the request, in a very special way, directed to the apostolic Holy See, of the creation of a Latin-American episcopal council, on the following bases:

1. CELAM will be composed of the representatives of the national episcopal conferences of Latin America, one representative being named for each conference.

2. Its functions will be: (a) to study the problems which concern the Church in Latin America; (b) coordinate activities; (c) promote and help Catholic endeavors; and (d) prepare new conferences of the Latin American episcopacy, when called by the Holy See."

CELAM works in very close liaison with the Holy See, the latter reserving to itself the right to revise statutes and by-laws, to control various activities, and a certain power of initiative. A pontifical commission for Latin America was created at Rome in 1958. Its purpose was to coordinate the activities of various Roman congregations concerned with that area, and it is charged with the relations between Rome and CELAM. The Curia has always possessed a greater power of control over ecclesiastical administration in Latin America than elsewhere, especially through the intervention of nuncios. When these nuncios are later promoted to similar posts in the old European nations, they often have great difficulty in adapting themselves to the more discreet role traditional in these countries. During the first session of the Council one of the more frequent complaints of Latin American bishops was the untimely interference of various nuncios. On the other hand, we ought to recognize the considerable wisdom on the part of the Holy See. As Cardinal Piazza affirmed in the name of Pius XII, this continental conference of the churches of South America had "neither precedent nor parallel in contemporary ecclesiastical history. We are dealing with a completely new experience." Bishops were brought together on the continental level, and organized a permanent organ of consultation among themselves. Since it was important that this experiment succeed, it was understandable that the Holy See kept a larger degree of control to guard against later developments.

One of the fruits of the Rio meeting was the episcopal conference held at Manila (Dec., 1958) under the presidency of Cardinal Agagianian of the Curia, sent by the pope, bringing together the bishops of the East and of Southeast Asia.

The third period opened at Rome the day of (or after) the solemn opening of the Second Vatican Council, when 2500 bishops present were asked to choose the members of the conciliar commissions. We recall the memorable intervention of Cardinals Lienart and Frings, who at the beginning of the Council asked the presidency (of which they were members) for a few days' delay for the purpose of consultation, so that they might make their choices with greater knowledge. It is hard to imagine the dismay many bishops had felt, especially those who came from far away and hardly knew anyone in the assembly. Spontaneously, the bishops who already belonged to an episcopal conference met at different colleges, convents, and hotels in Rome. This group movement by nationality and national or linguistic affinity encouraged other bishops to do the same. This consultation by national or regional groups was immediately approved by the Holy See, first, over the Vatican Radio, then in *Osservatore Romano,* and by the Pope himself.

Thus, the first plenary Assembly of the Italian episcopacy took place on October 15 under the presidency of Cardinal Siri. Italy had had episcopal conferences since 1849, especially in Umbria, but they were always limited to certain areas. In 1952 Pius XII established the Italian episcopal conference (CEI). This made provision for only two annual meetings, one for all the presidents of the twenty conciliar regions which comprise the Italian dioceses, and the second, just for cardinals. The nearness of Rome was always a psychological impediment to further development, and the Italian bishops were too numerous to make such meetings easy to run. During the Council the plenary Assembly of the Italian episcopacy continued to hold weekly meetings. There is no doubt that these regular sessions, although suffering from the rather authoritarian attitude of the president who did not allow much discussion, played a very important role in the growing awareness among Italian bishops of their episcopal responsibilities.

The creation of the African episcopal conference was even more important, regrouping nine regional conferences already existing or in the process of formation. The presidency was given to Cardinal Rugambwa, bishop of Bukoba; Mgr. Joan Zoa, archbishop of Yaoundé in Cameroun, and Mgr. Joseph Blomjous, bishop of Mwanza in Tanganyika, were the general secretaries, the former for French-speaking Africa, the latter for English-speaking Africa.

Several African bishops thought of taking advantage of their presence together in Rome to organize a first plenary Assembly of the African episcopacy. They wanted at the same time to prepare for the Council. Certain personalities in the Curia rejected the proposal on the pretext that it was improper to hold a particular council at the same time that the whole Church was preparing the Ecumenical Council. Events proved the African bishops right. Without this conference they would never have been able in so short a time to acquire the influence they did in fact exercise during the Council. In a few weeks their Conference was one of the best organized and most dynamic.

Before proceeding to the theological discussion of the problem, we ought to mention an important fact which, from the beginning, the problem of episcopal conferences clearly posed. In the Constitution on the Holy Liturgy the preparatory commission for the Liturgy mentioned episcopal conferences several times. It had even gone further. We have seen that according to pontifical tradition since Leo XIII, as incorporated in the Code of Canon Law, episcopal conferences did not possess any legislative power. This belonged properly only to a Council, either ecumenical or regional. Episcopal conferences are meetings of bishops who keep their diocesan autonomy intact but meet for consultation on common problems. In the schema on the Liturgy the preparatory commission confided the introduction of the vernacular in the liturgy to the competence of episcopal conferences. The text was formulated in this way: "It belongs to the competence of the episcopal conference of each region to decide on the limits and mode of use of the native language in the liturgy, subject to the approbation of the Holy See." The subcommission for amendment thought this text should be changed. It left to episcopal conferences the right henceforth to make proposals, while reserving to the Holy See the right to legislate. At the beginning several Fathers protested against this unexpected change in the text which did not seem to have been demanded by the Central Commission. At the end of the first session the initial text was approved by the Council almost unanimously, with only minor changes. In fact, the Council thus created a new ecclesial institution. This decision formally poses the question of the juridical and dogmatic nature of such an episcopal conference, which is very close to a regional council without possessing all its forms. The conciliar commission must have taken this into account. It dropped the name that one finds in the Code and which had been accepted in the first formulation of the schema. Probably in order to leave the door open for later conciliar precisions in this matter, the commission contented itself with a very general description of this new institution: "A regional meeting of bishops, legitimately constituted and competent."

The Practical Problem

The truth is that, strictly speaking, the Council could satisfy itself with a solution which would deliberately remain on the level of the concrete and practical necessities of the Church.

It is evident that it has often been impossible for a bishop to shut himself up within the limits of his diocese, and leave to the Holy See and the Roman Curia the responsibility for the organization and coordination of everything beyond the immediate problems of his ecclesiastical territory. What is done in one diocese can have serious repercussions in others of the same country, and even in other countries and continents. The existing difference of attitude among the bishops, for example, has often made for difficulties in regard to ecumenical relations. The same could be said on the political and social level.

The concrete problems posed nowadays on the national and international level call for a quick answer; because of this, or because they are related to a completely local situation, they cannot be adequately solved in Rome. The bishops therefore ought to consult one another out of necessity, and a great deal more frequently than before. When national and international organizations are being founded all over the world, it is regrettable that the Church, at least in some countries has so long been slow in admitting their usefulness.

Both outside the Church and within it laymen have often preceded their bishops in taking this direction. Modern pastoral necessities lead Rome to divide dioceses which have become too large or too populous, and this multiplication of dioceses makes their cohesion more necessary.

We could add a psychological reason. The day of his consecration the bishop receives the Holy Spirit. As we shall see later on, this divine guarantee is above all given to the episcopal college in communion with the Holy See. Some bishops occasionally have the tendency to believe that their consecration has placed them in direct contact with the Holy Spirit. They seem to forget that episcopal consecration is not a guarantee against the human influences of their education, social and national environment, temperament and theological formation. Regular meetings of bishops in a spirit of sincere and fraternal understanding could correct certain limitations, and even petty or eccentric opinions. The bishop who is hidden in episcopal solitude without any contacts but his immediate subordinates can be led to defend strange positions. He can only profit from the criticism of his colleagues.

In our time we see the necessity of giving greater importance to episcopal power. This reform, so urgent and necessary, rests on dogmatic requirements. Nevertheless, there are those who look on it with considerable apprehension; they are afraid that diocesan administration will take the place of Roman administration, a change not necessarily to the advantage of the Church. Distance, the realistic Italian temperament, and a long experience in diplomacy give the government of the Curia this suppleness and humanity which might not always be present in a diocesan curia. We see no other solution to this problem of human psychology than frequent episcopal meetings. A group of men arrives more easily at a nuanced view of things than a single individual, especially if the latter is isolated by his authority and the sacred character of his mission.

As in France and Latin America, this collaboration would allow for greater specialization. It is unnecessary to say that our modern problems, such as teaching, social questions, and ecumenism, are very complex. They presuppose knowledge of theology and canon law, as well as technical information, which every bishop cannot possess. It is impossible for a bishop to try to judge everything with expert knowledge. He ought to trust the judgment of specialists. He will do this more willingly if the expert is a colleague with whom he can speak frankly. It might be said that it should be possible for him to do this with any specialist, but we can easily understand that it will be easier with someone who also bears the responsibility of a bishop.

Nevertheless, episcopal conferences have one weakness which should not be ignored. Bishops remain perfectly equal among themselves and canonically independent of their colleagues. That is why decisions — or rather, common conclusions — of episcopal conferences have to be taken on a unanimous basis. When the bishops are very numerous, they may find it necessary to vote, but each bishop remains completely free. On returning to his own diocese, he may ignore the opinion of the majority of his colleagues. Every time the establishment of an episcopal conference has been proposed, this objection has been raised by one or several bishops. They fear that their diocesan autonomy is threatened.

It is obvious that the formula of unanimity often delays reforms that are absolutely necessary, especially in the smaller conferences, where a majority can never obtain a sufficient authority. That is why it has been the large conferences, well organized and with established commissions, that have made a greater impact.

It might be asked if canon law today does not already provide a basis for a provisional solution. As we have said, the code has an atomical view of the episcopacy. It was prepared at the end of the 19th century, and necessarily keeps all the theological weaknesses of that individualistic period. Episcopal collegiality has little place in theological and canonical preoccupations. The power of the bishop was limited only by the primacy of the pope, exercised through the medium of the Curia. There are certain links between the metropolitan bishop and his suffragans, but these only call for a certain collaboration on the administrative level. We are not speaking of the more extensive powers of the nuncio, at least in some countries, since to the degree that he has received a certain authority over the bishops of a country, he is no longer the diplomatic representative of the Holy See, but the instrument of pontifical authority.

The only practical solution seems to be for the bishops of a country or a continent voluntarily to give up some of their privileges and jurisdictional powers and confide them to the bishops as a whole, assembled in conference. This could be done consciously by a formal act, clearly delimiting the competence of the episcopal conference in that area, or implicitly by increasingly adopting an attitude of collaboration and mutual confidence. This is what happened in several episcopal conferences I mentioned, which since the war have played a decisive role in the religious history of a country or even a continent.

But as soon as the Council decides to confide a specific competence to episcopal conferences — for example, in the area of liturgy — it would seem that juridically this practical solution is inescapable. It does not in any way prejudge the question of a more profound foundation of this collegial competency. Receiving the mission from the Council to make decisions on the liturgy, episcopal conferences ought at least to accept, implicitly, a limitation of diocesan jurisdiction for the common good of an ecclesiastical region. It would be strange to think that the Council's intention was to reserve this competence to occasions when there was complete unanimity among all the members of a conference, with each bishop able to maintain his own point of view against the opinion of his colleagues. This is certainly not the intention contained in the reform of the liturgy, which desires unity in diversity but not liturgical anarchy. The discussions on liturgy during the first session have shown that as soon as there is a question of a concrete application in this matter, there are as many opinions as bishops present. This is true for every liturgical reform, where the richness of sacramental symbolism implies a large variety of practical solutions.

Episcopal conferences, once invested with this power, inevitably call for the only human way by which a group with equal authority can reach unity of action — that is, a vote. As long as a majority remains incapable of gaining a decision, it seems pointless to give episcopal conferences any real authority. The impossibility of a decisive vote and the necessity of unanimity is perfectly understandable for a completely consultative body. It becomes absurd when this conference is given a real power of jurisdiction over a determined territory. The term *statuere,* used by the conciliar commission in the first chapter of the Constitution on the Liturgy, and finally adopted by the Council at the close of the first session — has a precise meaning in ecclesiastical law. It signifies an act of authority, and hence also includes the exercise of the power of episcopal jurisdiction.

Dogmatic Foundations

But is it necessary to reach an agreement on the dogmatic foundations of this canonical authority given to episcopal conferences by the Council? During the first session, there were bishops, theologians and even observers who regretted that the Council had opened with the discussion of such practical problems as pastoral and liturgical adaptation, instead of dealing with theory and principles. I believe that this way of attacking problems was providential, allowing the Council to find internal cohesion and its own climate within a few weeks. Nevertheless, some would have preferred, at least in the beginning, to see the Council firmly establish the doctrinal bases of episcopal power before taking up various concrete applications.

Such an attitude is an illusion, and seems to show a misunderstanding of the true nature and history of the Church. If one wants to be a good theologian, he can never know Church history too well. The Church is not a system, but a living organism, adapting itself to the conditions of times and places. The internal law of its life is the Holy Spirit, who has no desire to impose legalistic or conceptual immobility, but inspires the Church to continual reform in a changing world. The Holy Spirit also preserves the Church from betraying its inner substance in the course of its evolution. The life-substance, which the Church has received from its divine Founder, is never possessed as a definitive acquisition of its own, but is continually given to the Church by its Head, Jesus Christ, and by the Holy Spirit.

In the Church life has always preceded theological reflection and canonical structures. This was true of the fundamental mysteries of our faith, the Trinity and the Incarnation. We find the same phenomenon in regard to sacramental life. The *praxis ecclesiae* is one of the principle sources of inspiration for dogmatic theology; it has always been an important *locus theologicus*.

That is why it seems urgent for the Council to specify a few concrete applications of episcopal power rather than immediately tackle the arduous and disputed problem of the ultimate nature of episcopal power. There is an element of rationalism in this impatience for definition, a lack of respect for the laws of growth which determine theological reflection in the Church or in any communitarian and human thinking. The true problems should ripen slowly in an open and positive discussion, not in controversy which only hardens positions. They should ripen above all through the process of living experience. A few very specific decrees of the Council on the personal and collegial exercise of episcopal power in dialogue and communion of faith with the see of Peter will do more to attain equilibrium between primacy and episcopacy — for which so many Christians look to the Council — than dogmatic definitions which would inevitably remain vague and ambiguous. After a century of the exercise of episcopal responsibility on a larger and more active field than after Vatican I, theology will find it easy to reflect on the nature and source of this responsibility in the Church. It is obvious that canon law, enlightened both by theological reflection and the experience of the life of the Church, will be better able to establish juridical structures for the delicate aspects of relations between episcopacy and the primacy, and the relations of bishops among themselves and with their priests and faithful.

This does not mean that we should abandon reflection on this subject as worthless: the main studies on the episcopacy in recent years prove the opposite. There is an enormous positive work to do: the study of Scripture to find a better understanding of relevant New Testament texts, reading them against the background of the ancient tradition of the Hebrews, without neglecting the

Qumran sects. We do not yet know enough of the tradition of the Fathers and the history of the liturgy and law of ordination, but there are studies going on to which we can only refer.

At this moment it seems that there are two opposed currents of thought in the Church, with different conceptions of the sacrament of holy orders. But if we look at this division more deeply, we will discover an over-all view of the Church which, while retaining the common truths of faith, arranges them in a very different way.

There is a conception of the Church which could be called pyramidal, in which all ecclesiastical power seems concentrated in the person of the pope, the summit of this hierarchial pyramid. The ultimate reason for this is that he is the vicar of Christ on earth. This term, which has known various meanings in theological history, is taken in a strong sense. All other forms of ecclesial authority are communicated in the Church by means of this hierarchical pyramid, which is looked at primarily from a juridical point of view. We are not thinking of the simple power of jurisdiction, proper to every established and perfect society, but of the real power of authority as vicar, exercised in the name and as the instrument of the Lord Jesus. Such a conception of the Church and its essential structures is papalist and encourages centralization.

These theologians give such importance to this form of ecclesiastical jurisdiction that they reduce the power of holy orders in the strict sense to the power of sacramental sanctification. This was the tradition of several medieval scholastics, although if their reasoning is followed carefully, a more nuanced theological synthesis will be discovered. But under the influence of a faulty interpretation of Trent, some theologians believe that this position was defined as a dogma of faith. (This is again to forget that Trent never wished to give an exhaustive doctrine of faith, especially on the sacraments; it only defended those points of doctrine belonging to the common doctrine of the Church which were attacked by the Lutherans.) For them the power of orders in the strict sense is above all the power to consecrate bread and wine and thereby to offer the sacrifice of the Mass. Frequently they will add the power to absolve sins, and to administer the other sacraments. In such a theology the power of orders of a bishop is almost identical with that of the priest. The bishop reserves ordination to himself, and in the West, confirmation. But since these are looked on as notable exceptions, this power of episcopal consecration is only an "ordinary" power, which in certain cases can be exercised by a priest. This extraordinary exercise of power can only be conceded by the pope — which, moreover, does not correspond completely with the facts of history — and we see again how in such a theology of the Church and of holy orders, the strictly priestly power is always subject to the power of jurisdiction of the vicar, exercised in the name of Christ.

In this view of the Church episcopal conferences cannot be invested with authority except by an express delegation of authority by the Holy Father. The pope freely surrenders a part of his power of immediate jurisdiction over all the Church in order to delegate it to recognized and competent episcopal conferences. The logical implication of this way of thinking is that such conferences would exercise a delegated pontifical power, not its own episcopal power. (We do not say that this opinion is explicitly defended by all who hold this general position but it does seem to be part of the logic of their approach.)

It is this theological tradition which is primarily responsible for what I have called the atomic concept of the episcopacy, as it seems to be defined in canon law. The bishop has proper authority only over his own territory. He does not have any authority outside his territory, except in certain cases over his own diocesans who may be outside the territorial limits of his authority. Only the pope possesses an immediate episcopal jurisdiction of his own over the whole Church. But it is obvious that in an episcopal conference each bishop, as a member of the conference, participates immediately in the authority exercised over a territory which is not his own. The Code knows only one case in which the bishop can exercise an authority over the whole

Church — that is, in an Ecumenical Council. But apart from an Ecumenical Council, bequeathed to us by ancient tradition, the Code — like those theologians we just mentioned — recognizes only a territorial authority in a bishop, at most an authority linked to a definite group of persons. Logically, it would be necessary to conclude that the authority of episcopal conferences, which clearly differ from Ecumenical Councils, is closer to pontifical power than episcopal power. That is why the supporters of this theory seem less favorable to the extension of episcopal power by the concession of an enlarged and well-defined competence to episcopal conferences.

If the first view of the Church suggests a pyramid, because papalist and centralized — and consequently curial — resting above all on the power of jurisdiction, the other view suggests the image of concentric circles.

In it we do not start with the pope, but with the people of God, the Body of Christ and his Spouse. This Church is the community of the faithful, obedient to Christ its Lord, assembled by the Father in the strength of the Spirit. Pope, bishops, and priests are first of all members of the faithful. They remain so all their lives. On this fundamental level of faith and charity they do not differ from the other members of the Church, all consecrated children of God by baptism and confirmation.

Within this churchly body, which is also a priestly body because sacramentally united to Christ the Priest, certain members have received a specific mission conferred upon them at ordination. The mission does not raise them above the others, but consecrates them to their service; they receive a mission as part of the *diaconie*, the ministry.

In this view of the Church the power of holy orders is emphasized rather than jurisdiction, which by the same token becomes more limited and restricted. In fact, it does not seem that the power of holy orders ought to be limited to the administration of sacraments. By its essence it is a mission which participates in the plenitude of the Mission of Christ. It was realized preeminently in the mission of the apostles, the foundation of every ministry of the Church. This mission includes a function of sanctification and authority, the ministry of act and of word. If we speak constantly of *diaconie*, it is to remain closer to the biblical doctrine and to avoid any kind of metaphysical clericalism, based on an unfortunate ontology of the priestly character. But we do not wish to deny that this mission and function are real. They are the foundation, if not the ultimate basis, of sacramental efficacity. The power of jurisdiction, on the other hand, has no other purpose than to organize the exercise of this mission in the life of the Church. In the last analysis, jurisdiction never establishes a power in the Church, but applies it concretely and determines the conditions of its exercise.

This mission is confided to the episcopal college, the heir of the college of the apostles. Within this college the pope, a bishop like "his brothers in the episcopacy," has received a mission and therefore also a real unifying function, the pontifical primacy. Priests are essentially collaborators of the bishop, and participate in his mission, and hence in some of his functions act in union with him. Because they are ordained as *cooperatores ordinis nostri*, their strictly priestly mission rests on their ordination; the extent and concrete forms of participation of this priestly mission are determined by the power of jurisdiction. Thus, by his ordination a priest fundamentally possesses the power to absolve sins, but he can exercise it validly and licitly in the western Church only after he has been given jurisdiction by the bishop.

In this theology of the Church, the relations between the power of order and that of jurisdiction are very different from those we found in the theology previously analyzed. The order constitutes what we should call the substance, the metaphysical substratum of this mission, while the pontifical or episcopal jurisdiction governs its varied applications on the level of the concrete, according to the conditions of place and time. That is why the essential structure of the Church cannot change, but the forms of application of this fundamental structure have been and will be varied, always open to new applications and reforms.

It is in the power of order that we should see the foundations for the authority of episcopal conferences. By his consecration the bishop has been joined to the episcopal college, invested with the plenitude of the episcopal mission, which participates in that of the apostles. Hence by virtue of his consecration every bishop possesses a universal function for the whole Church. Nevertheless, this function differs from that of the pope. The latter possesses in his primacy a direct and immediate episcopal mission over the whole Church; it is attached to his person as symbol of unity and image of Christ. The bishop possesses this universal mission only as a member of the episcopal college. On the existential level he can exercise this mission only in union with the other bishops and with the Holy See.

Ecclesiastical law, therefore, ought to define on the concrete level the different juridical forms which would permit bishops to exercise collegially this universal mission. But even then order takes priority over jurisdiction, charism over law. The bishops ought always to feel themselves responsible before the whole Church; on the existential level, they should never believe themselves dispensed from the duty to "live in communion" with their brothers in the episcopacy. The personal, existential acceptance of this universal mission seems to us even more important than the different institutionalized forms which will also be necessary. Charism is always more important than law, but law makes its exercise more constant and efficacious. It is therefore necessary for the Church to create in the course of time various adapted juridical forms which will allow the episcopal college to exercise this mission.

The Ecumenical Council is the most striking and solemn manifestation of this mission of the episcopacy. The history of Councils confirms my theory. The structure of Councils has often varied, and will have to evolve further, but their "substance" remains the same — to be the visible expression at a given moment and in one place in the world of this universal mission of the episcopacy. Regional and provincial councils, also belonging to an old tradition, are another. Episcopal conferences, whether national or continental, are a third. Still others can be found.

In this view of the Church the foundation of the authority of episcopal conferences does not rest in an explicit or implicit delegation of power from the Holy Father. It seems to us that during the pontificate of Pius XII the Curia thought in these terms, at least on the occasion of the foundation and direction of new episcopal conferences on the continental level. The authority of an episcopal conference rests on the consecration of each bishop, and on the fundamental fact that by this consecration he is henceforth part of the episcopal college instituted by Christ. Participation in an episcopal conference, therefore, belongs to the normal exercise of the bishop's authority. It is not necessary that its decisions be formally approved by the Holy See. This approbation is one of the possible forms of communion which ought to exist between the episcopal college and the primate, but history knows others, such as the "letters of peace" sent by the pope on receiving the decrees of an ecumenical or particular council. It is evident that the pope or the ecumenical council can determine the concrete modalities of the exercise of his authority. Hence we again find ourselves on the level of the ecclesiastical "economy" — the level of concrete applications and of law. It also seems that the pope has the power to limit this exercise of power when the unity of the Church is endangered.

One last remark as a conclusion. This theology of the Church has been elaborated in recent years in Europe under the influence of biblical, patristic, ecumenical and liturgical renewal. All this relates to theology. That is why we do not think that the Council is in a position to formulate dogmatic definitions on the episcopacy which take into account these multiple aspects of ecclesiology. It is very probable that these questions are not yet ready to be resolved. We would give more importance to life; it is in its life that the Church will discover its deepest nature.

Nevertheless, it is remarkable that those very European bishops who favor a dogmatic declaration on the nature of the episcopacy are often refractory to any idea of strengthening the authority of episcopal conferences. They are afraid that their own powers will be limited by those of others. They do not want to accept the possibility of even indirect influence by their colleagues in their own affairs. This contradiction between abstract ideas and existential attitudes shows once more that there is a considerable difference between theological speculation and practical life. If their ideas are new — and, as people say, progressive — their attitude is frankly conservative.

In the young churches, on the contrary, we find almost the opposite. Their theological ideas are rather conservative, but in practice urgent pastoral problems force them to look for new and sometimes daring formulas. Thus, during the Council the bishops of Latin America, Africa, and Asia complained of not being able to meet European bishops except in their different national episcopal conferences. There is no over-all episcopal conference for Europe. Our bishops, often very enlightened theologically, still remain too much enclosed in their various nationalisms. Europe searches for its unity, but one cannot say that our bishops provide much of an example.

Related Problems

The establishment of episcopal conferences with a real competence and authority would offer other advantages for the Church which we have not yet mentioned. It would improve the relations between the Curia and the world episcopacy, among the bishops themselves, and of bishops with religious and laymen.

During the preparation of the Council an old complaint emerged, which has been raised at every Council since Basle and Constance; the Curia must be internationalized. This is true, especially at this moment of history when the Church is confronted with a planetary civilization. It is ridiculous to want to run the Church by Italian usages, as is the case in planning the system of ecclesiastical study, or allowing for special sensibilities on the Index, the love of clerical display, the suspicion of laymen, and the obsession with Communism. On the other hand, we should free ourselves from illusions in this area. During the Council Cardinal Ottaviani frequently remarked that the Sacred

Congregation of the Holy Office was the most international of all the Roman congregations. It is a fact of experience that foreigners who live in Rome for a long time frequently become more Roman than the Romans. They do not possess that fundamental realism and sense of diplomacy which is both the strength and weakness of Italian prelates.

It would be better to talk of "decurializing" the Curia if this too were not an illusion, and even a piece of nonsense. The Curia is essentially a corps of specialists in ecclesiastical administration, who are to assist the pope in the exercise of his primacy. Without the Curia, the pope is paralyzed. It is impossible for him personally to study and keep up with all the affairs which are sent to Rome. Besides, those concerned exclusively with administration — at least as an organized body — are bound to take on some of the attitudes of bureaucrats. Let us be realistic; the Curia ought to remain what it is, and remaining what it is, it cannot help but become "curial."

The Council has made us see that the Curia would be different if there were organized bodies it had to treat as equals. This would help to solve another complaint of bishops that on their visits to Rome they feel they are treated as junior employees who must give an account of their administration. The real source of our trouble is that there is now almost no possibility of open discussion between the episcopacy and the Curia. During the Council the prelates of the Curia had to treat their colleagues in the episcopacy as equals. Both groups profited enormously from this experience. It has helped us to a true conception of authority, which is never a one-way street. God's will does not come down from heaven vertically, but manifests itself through an open and confident dialogue within the Church, whose act of authority is only the authentic conclusion of that dialogue.

It is evident that the Curia, to the degree that it more immediately represents the will of the pope, possesses an authority over the bishops. But the Curia should also be the means by which an exchange between the primacy and the world episcopacy takes place. It therefore cannot do without the frank and unrestricted expression of opinion by the bishops. It is illusory to expect this openness and concern from any curia, whether Italian or international, if it only has to deal with individual bishops. An exchange of views in such circumstances is almost impossible. On the one side there is a group of routine-ridden specialists, on the other there is a single man, often overburdened with work, handicapped by his position as petitioner — he has a favor to obtain, or even financial assistance — and in most cases having no practical experience of Roman administrative practices.

A real exchange between the Curia and the episcopacy will take place only if the bishops can address themselves to Rome through the intermediary of their episcopal conferences. The latter must not become an extension of the Curia into foreign countries, but should possess real authority. There will be bishops specializing in the various problems of pastoral action and canon law, designated for that purpose by their colleagues.

We are not thinking of a bishops' union, but an organ for an encounter and exchange of views on the level of equality between the Curia and the episcopacy. The Curia should stay what it is, but should put itself at the service of the only authorities founded by Christ, the primate and the episcopacy in communion with the Holy See. The Curia is simply an ecclesiastical institution, and only has meaning in such a spirit of service. It must render this service, but with our present system it is impossible, even with the best intentions: it is a question of psychology.

Episcopal conferences would also be able to improve relations between the different members of the world episcopacy. This deeper communion is part of the very life of the Church. During its first centuries the bishops considered the maintenance of these multiple contacts as one of the most serious obligations of their charge. It was the only way of keeping the Church's unity intact and living. In recent centuries we have become accustomed to hand over this responsibility to the Holy See.

The maintenance of their relations goes beyond the possibilities of a single bishop. It is by the intermediary of episcopal conferences, especially on a continental level, that the bishops will be able to rediscover their communion in faith and charity. This has already happened. The German bishops' project, Misereror, the seminaries for Latin America founded by European bishops, the sending of diocesan priests to Africa or Latin America, the establishment of schools on these continents, sustained by funds and personnel of European bishops — all these things have been done through CELAM and the African conferences. But in these cases episcopal conferences should also possess a definite authority. A simple organ of consultation is not enough.

We should also consider the place of the religious orders. The increasing emphasis on episcopal authority has sometimes given the impression that it would be at their expense. During the preparation for the Council a joke went the rounds that the Curia would never surrender any of its privileges, but would hand over the religious orders to the bishops to appease their desire for power. The fact is that the practice of some diocesan curias would make one think that the only evil from which the Church suffers is that the bishops cannot do as they please with the religious orders.

Let us be realistic; obviously, the exemptions of religious are in need of revision, just as many other things in the Church. They too should be adapted to the conditions of modern life. But to reform or adapt is not the same thing as to abolish.

The principle of exemption has a positive sense. By exemption the orders are not only detached from the authority of the local bishop — with excellent restrictions anticipated by the Code — but are linked more directly to the central authority of the Church, in the Holy See. That is why most of the heads of orders reside at Rome, in direct contact with the pope and the Curia. Priests are ordained as collaborators of the bishop, or rather of the episcopacy. One group of priests accepts this collaboration in intimate liaison with the local bishop — these are diocesan priests. Another group places itself at the service of the episcopacy, while remaining at the disposition of the Holy See. For this division of work there are reasons both of simple tactics and human prudence. To preserve the availability of priestly service, one ought to be able to form and send priests freely, wherever their need is felt. The immense effort for the evangelization of the world has been the work of religious orders. They are also often prepared for specialized tasks, like teaching, the care of the sick, the preaching of retreats. All of this appropriate formation and mobility would be lost if in each diocese the local bishop could interfere in everything regarding the formation of members, the division of work, and the assignment of workers.

Episcopal conferences could help toward a solution in this matter as well. It is noteworthy that everywhere that episcopal conferences have been established, there has also arisen an Assembly of the superiors of religious orders. Every time these two organisms succeed in collaborating in their own common love of the Church, most of the problems raised by exemptions tend to disappear. Why should we want to resolve everything by means of authority? There is a certain simplism, and an overly human view of episcopal authority, in thinking it lessened if there are limits in the exercise of its authority. Both bishops and religious superiors ought to leave behind their suspicious particularisms. Superiors should continually recall that before being a member of a religious order, proud of its tradition and faithful to its Rule and its religious spirit, they are members of the Church. Moreover, this was always the major preoccupation of the great founders; religious particularism was not part of their spiritual tradition. That is the work of their successors, who are overly concerned with good administration. It often rests on a legalistic formalism, an excessive devotion to the Rule, especially when it is forgotten that the Rule has no meaning apart from the Gospel, of which it is a particular expression.

In any case it would be impossible to have all the religious orders dependent on local ordinaries. This would be their death. But it is quite another thing to work for direct and open collaboration with the episcopal conferences of a single country, and especially of a single continent.

Let me add a few words on the relations of laymen with their bishops. We often hear laymen complaining that their bishops stay shut up in their little diocesan curias, jealously guarded by a small group of collaborators who are no longer young and often uninterested in what goes on outside the episcopal palace. Solitude remains the greatest danger of our bishops. Meanwhile laymen increasingly feel the necessity of intense collaboration on the national and international level. The newspapers are always full of the same thing. Europe has recovered after two world wars by means of collaboration. In addition, laymen travel much more than a century ago. They visit other countries on vacation, and inevitably make contact with religious life in these countries. They want the Church to follow the movement which is bringing men closer together. One can understand how the often narrow parochialism of some diocesan curias disturbs them, strengthening the already common impression that the Church belongs to another age and is incapable of adapting itself to modern life.

It is obvious that regular episcopal conferences would permit bishops to keep up with what is going on, enlarge their perspectives, and hear what is being done in other dioceses and other countries. If these conferences possessed a real competence, they would be able to unify religious life in a country in an efficacious manner. We have only to think of the difficulties encountered by those who wish public prayers in the vernacular unified for all countries using the same language. It is often the bishops or their immediate collaborators in the diocesan curias who are attached to a national — if not nationalistic — particularism, which is foreign to our age and has no meaning in the Church. We insist on our obligations of charity and collaboration. Episcopal conferences would manifest to all that the bishops are the first to give the example, even if they have to sacrifice their local habits for this purpose, attacking a narrowness which frequently lessens the influence of the pious. In other words, the conferences will be a real testimony of catholicity and unity. It is God's appeal to our age.

Epilogue

POPE PAUL'S ADDRESS AT THE OPENING OF THE SECOND SESSION OF THE ECUMENICAL COUNCIL*

WE WELCOME you, dearest brothers in Christ, called from every country of the world where the holy Catholic Church has established her hierarchy. We welcome you who have responded so readily to Our invitation to be here with Us for the Second Vatican Council's second session, which We have the happiness of inaugurating today under the protection of Michael the Archangel, champion of the Christian people.

How well does the noble and predestined title of *Church* apply to this meeting of brothers, this "community," this "convocation" of men joyously assembled from East and West, from North and South. The sight of you here seems to give added meaning to a scriptural text which is in Our mind today: "The utterance fills every land, the message reaches the ends of the world" (Rom 10:13; Ps 18:5).

Those two sublime marks of the Church, her unity and catholicity, are here indeed most marvelously combined.

But this spectacle of the Church's universality leads Us on to think not merely of her apostolic origin, portrayed and proclaimed by this assembly, but also of the aim of this Church we love so well: the aim of God's Church to make all men saints. These are the distinguishing marks of the Church, and they are here for all to see. The Church is here, the radiant Spouse of Christ. Our hearts are inflamed with the certain, yet ever hidden, assurance of being indeed the mystical body of Christ, and ours is the matchless joy — hidden as yet from the world — that is born of

---

* Reprinted from *The Pope Speaks*.

that utterance: "Gracious the sight and full of comfort, when brethren dwell united" (Ps 132:1).

What a joy it is for Us to contemplate the first effects of this human yet divine event which is unfolding at this very moment before Our eyes. For we are reassembled now as in another cenacle — a magnificent building indeed, yet hardly large enough to hold the multitude of those who are gathered here together. Assuredly, Christ's Virgin Mother Mary has taken her place in our midst, and you, dear brothers, are gathered here around Us, the successor of Peter the Apostle, the last and least to share his office and authority. And you too are apostles, drawing your origin from the college of apostles whose true heirs you are.

Here we pray together, united in the same faith, the same love. Here we have the assurance of a heavenly gift, the Holy Spirit present among us, inspiring us, teaching us, strengthening us. Here the tongues of every nation join in one common utterance, framing the message that must go out to the whole wide world. Here with unfaltering steps the pilgrim Church has come together after twenty centuries of journeying through the world. Pilgrim bands of apostles have come here from every corner of the globe to seek refreshment, to assuage their thirst, to find new heart for the work that lies ahead; when leaving here they go out into the world once more and into time, to toil for things that are beyond this world, beyond all time.

We welcome you, dearest brothers. This welcome you receive from one who is the least among you, God's servant of servants, bearer though he be of the keys of sovereignty given by Jesus Christ to Peter. It is thus that he thanks you for your tokens of obedience and loyalty, and truly expresses his desire to join you in prayer and conversation, in your deliberations and endeavors. Here, at the very beginning of this great Council's second session, We call the immortal God to witness that Our mind repudiates all thought of human sovereignty, all ambitions for personal power. Instead, Our only thought and desire, brothers, is to obey the divine command which has placed Us in the midst of you all as your supreme Shepherd. Of you that command requires that

you be Our *joy* and *crown,* a *communion of saints.* It calls for
your loyalty toward Us, your friendship and co-operation. And
We in turn, with all Our heart, give you Our devotion, Our
esteem, Our loyalty and Our love.

In accordance with time-honored tradition We had intended
to send you an inaugural encyclical. But why, We asked Ourself, should We put down in writing what, by a fortunate and
unique opportunity, We could communicate to you by word of
mouth here at this Ecumenical Council? True, We cannot now
tell you everything that is in Our mind, and much that We have
to say could be more easily dealt with in writing. Nevertheless,
what We say now may serve to introduce not only this meeting,
but Our pontificate as well. Let Our very own words, then, take
the place of an encyclical, which, with God's help, We will write
you later, when these busy days are over.

And now, having welcomed you, Our next task surely must
be to introduce Ourself. For We are new to the pontifical office
which We hold, or rather, which We are but now entering upon.
As of course you know, on last June 20th, the feast of the Sacred
Heart of Jesus, the college of cardinals (here present; and We
rejoice to make known to them once more Our allegiance and
devotion) thought fit to disregard Our human frailty and elect Us
to the episcopal See of Rome, and thus to the supreme pontificate
of the Universal Church.

But as We cast Our mind back, We cannot but recall the vivid
memory of Our predecessor of glorious and immortal fame,
John XXIII, whom we loved so dearly. To Us and to all who
were privileged to see him seated in this chair which now We
occupy, his very name brings back the remembrance of his wonderful, priestly presence here last October 11th, when he opened
the first session of his Second Ecumenical Vatican Council and
gave that address which was acclaimed not only by the Church,
but by the whole of human society, as the inspired utterance of
a prophet of our times. That speech still rings in Our ears. It still
lives on in Our consciousness, and shows clearly the direction
which this Council must take. It dispels all hesitation from our

minds, all the weariness that may overtake us on this difficult road.

Dear, revered Pope John! What gratitude, what recognition is not due to you for having been inspired to call this Council, implementing your resolve to open out new pathways for the Church, and to water the earth with the teaching and grace of Jesus Christ in new, fair-flowing, still uncharted streams! What prompted you to take up again the broken threads of the First Vatican Council? This world was not the spur. No single earthly circumstances demanded it. It was Heaven's inspiration, and your own insight into the groping, aching needs of this our age. There were some who thought that the former Council's recognition of the sovereign power conferred by Jesus Christ on the Roman Pontificate was sufficient for the ruling of the Church, and did away with the need for ecumenical councils. But by your action you yourself took the initiative in dispelling this unjustifiable assumption.

Your purpose in calling the brothers together was not just to resume studies interrupted before, and to continue legislation held in abeyance, but to make these successors of the Apostles realize their corporate unity with the Sovereign Pontiff, and derive from him strength and leadership to safeguard "the sacred heritage of Christian truth, and to expound it with greater efficacy."

With this more exalted aim of the Council you combined a pastoral aim, which at this present time would seem to be even more urgent and rewarding. "We are not here," you said, "primarily to discuss certain fundamentals of Catholic doctrine . . . but to study them afresh, and reformulate them in contemporary terms."

As for those things which go to make up the teaching of the Church, you confirmed the opinion that an article of Christian doctrine is not merely a truth to be investigated by reason in the light of faith, but is also an efficacious, life-giving Word. The task of Church authority is not just to condemn errors which pervert the truth, but also to proclaim her wealth of positive and vital teaching. And since the Church's magisterial authority is not wholly speculative nor purely negative, this Council must do more and more to demonstrate the power and dynamic quality of Christ's teaching; for it was Christ who said: "The words I have been speaking to you are spirit and life" (Jn 6:64).

We are not, therefore, going to forget the exceedingly wise directives that you gave us in your capacity as foremost Father of this Council, and which we now recall to mind: ". . . Our duty is not just to guard this treasure (Catholic doctrine), as though it were some museum-piece and we the curators, but earnestly and fearlessly to dedicate ourselves to the work that needs to be done in this modern age of ours, pursuing the path which the Church has followed for almost twenty centuries." Hence ". . . we must work out ways and means of expounding these truths in a manner more consistent with a predominantly pastoral view of the Church's teaching office."

Nor will we overlook that other supremely important issue: the unity of all believers in Christ who wish to belong to His Church, our Father's house — to use, John, your own words — the doors of which are opened wide for all the world to enter. May this coming second session of the Ecumenical Council, which you organized and inaugurated, faithfully follow the direction you have given it, and be enabled, with God's help, to achieve those aims which you most ardently desired and prayed for.

And so, dear brothers, we must carry on as we have begun. But in manifesting this intention of Ours, We are put in mind of a further consideration, which is so supremely important that We cannot fail to mention it before this whole assembly, even though you are well aware of it and, indeed, wholly influenced by it.

What, dear brothers, are we going to make our starting-point? What path must we tread if we are going to be guided by God's law rather than by any reasons so far expounded? What goal are we to set ourselves? For though our strivings during this time on earth must inevitably take account of the temporal conditions of this mortal life, they must nevertheless be directed always toward man's destined final end after this earthly pilgrimage.

These three questions — easy enough to understand, but nevertheless of supreme importance — have one and the same answer:

Christ. We who are gathered here together on this solemn occasion have to remind ourselves of this, and proclaim it to the whole world. Christ is our starting-point, Christ our leader and our way, Christ our hope and our goal.

May this Ecumenical Council have a clear realization of that bond which binds us to Jesus Christ — a bond that is one yet manifold, stringent yet compelling, mysterious yet manifest, tightly drawn yet most welcome. It binds us, the living, holy Church, to Christ from whom we come, through whom we live, toward whom we tend. May this our present assembly shine with no other light than Christ, the light of the world. May our minds seek no other truth than that proclaimed by the words of the Lord, our only teacher. May our sole ambition be to give whole-hearted, loyal obedience to His commands. May no other confidence sustain us than that which strengthens our own poor frailty — relying on His words: "And behold I am with you all through the days that are coming, until the consummation of the world" (Mt 28:20).

If only in this glorious hour We could find words adequate to express the praises of our Lord Jesus Christ! We make Our own those words of the sacred liturgy:

> *You alone, Christ, satisfy*
> *All our mind; to you we cry,*
> *Longingly, with heart sincere,*
> *Confident that you will hear.*

As We recite these words, Jesus Himself seems to stand before Us, clothed, dear brothers of the Eastern Church, in the majestic splendor of the Pantocrator portrayed in your basilicas — and in some Western basilicas too — and We gaze at Him in awe and wonder. Indeed, We see Ourself in the role of Pope Honorius III as depicted in wonderful mosaic in the apse of St. Paul's basilica outside the city walls, worshipping Christ. He lies there a small, seemingly lifeless figure, prostrate on the ground, kissing Christ's feet. And Christ towers above him in regal, majestic splendor, the Master benevolently presiding over the assembled community — in the basilica, as in the Church.

But the vision conjured up before Our eyes is no mere mural, no mere subject of pictorial artistry. It is a reality — here, in this assembly of ours, where Christ is acknowledged as the wellspring of man's redemption, the head of the Church; and where the Church is recognized as the earthly yet mystical dimension and extension of Christ. In imagination We see that vision described by the Apostle John: "He shewed me, too, a river, whose waters give life; it flows, clear as crystal, from the throne of God, from the throne of the Lamb" (Ap 22:1).

We think it wholly fitting that this Council should make this vision — or rather, this mystic celebration — its starting point. It is a celebration which proclaims our Lord Jesus Christ as the Word incarnate, Son of God and Son of Man, the world's redeemer. He indeed is the hope of the human race, its one supreme teacher and shepherd, our bread of life, our High Priest and our victim, the one mediator between God and men, the savior of this world and king of the eternal world to come. It is a celebration, too, which shows us to be divinely called by Christ, His disciples, apostles, witnesses, ministers and envoys, and, together with the rest of the faithful, living members of that one, great, mystical body which by faith and sacraments He fashions for Himself throughout the long-continued ages of mankind: His Church, a visible yet spiritual society, fraternal and hierarchical, temporal now, yet destined to endure forever.

This, dear brothers, is a truth of supreme importance. Christ is invisibly yet really our founder and our head. All that we have we receive from Him, and with Him we form, as St. Augustine said, the *Christus totus,* the whole Christ. This realization underlies the whole of Christian teaching about the Church. If we weigh it carefully we will surely gain a clearer insight into the principal aims of this Council. For the sake of clarity and brevity We will summarize these aims under four headings: (1) The notion, or, if you prefer it, the awareness of the Church; (2) Her renewal; (3) The restoration of unity among all Christians; (4) The Church's dialogue with the men of our own day.

I

THE NOTION OF THE CHURCH

First, then, there can be no doubt of the existence in the Church of a keen desire to come at least to a full understanding of her true nature. Indeed, this desire is forced upon her by very necessity and her obvious duty. We are all of us well aware of the lovely images used in Scripture to describe the Church's nature. In various places the Church is called Christ's building, the house of God, His temple and tabernacle, His people, His flock, His vineyard, field and city, Christ's bride and mystical body. The very richness of this wonderful imagery impelled the Church to proclaim herself a visible, hierarchical society, founded on this earth, yet animated by some inner, mysterious power. Pope Pius XII's magnificent encyclical *Mystici Corporis* went some way to satisfy the Church's desire to give a full account of herself. It also stimulated keener theological thought in the Church, aimed at reaching a specific and fully satisfactory definition of the Church's nature.

This theme had in fact been on the agenda for the First Vatican Council, and many external factors have impelled theologians, both inside and outside the Catholic Church, to give it their special attention. Among such factors We may mention the growth in social relationships which characterizes the contemporary scene, increased communications between men, and the need to judge the various Christian denominations in accordance with a true and universally valid notion founded on divine revelation.

The Christian religion has been in existence for almost two thousand years, during which time the Catholic Church has extended everywhere, as have also other communions which take their name from Christ and are called Churches. Even so, it need cause no surprise that the true, definitive and complete notion of the Church as founded by Christ and begun by the Apostles still lacks more precise formulation. For the Church is a mystery, a mystic reality, steeped in the presence of God. It is always, therefore, possible to gain new and deeper insights into its nature.

It is the nature of the human mind to advance in thought and learning. From the apprehension of empirical truths it rises to a higher, more scientific understanding of those truths, which in turn, by a logical process of deduction, gives rise to the knowledge of further truths. And when the mind is confronted with a complex reality, yet one which is possessed of primary certitude, it pauses to consider the various aspects of this truth, one after another. We thus have that development in the activity of the enquiring mind to which history bears constant witness.

And We are convinced that the time has now come for a more thorough investigation into the truth which concerns the Church. This truth must be subjected to a more intensive examination, and formulated — not, perhaps, as a solemn, dogmatic pronouncement — but certainly in declarations expressing in a clearer and more authoritative form the Church's teaching about herself.

The Church's self-awareness increases with her unswerving adherence to the thought and utterances of Christ, her reverence for the proven precepts of sacred Tradition, and her response to the inner guidance of the Holy Spirit. It is He who now seems to be urging the Church to make every effort to gain the recognition of all men for what she is.

All the indications lead Us to believe that in this Council the truth-giving Spirit will shed a brighter radiance over the sacred ranks of the teaching Church, and inspire a clearer doctrine regarding the Church's nature. The Church, too, gazing in the reflection of herself in the face of Christ, her Bridegroom, and impelled by ardent love, will strive to realize the beauty that is hers, the radiant beauty that Christ looks for in His Church.

Thus the main theme of this second session of the Ecumenical Council will be the Church. A thorough investigation must be made into her inner nature, with a view to defining this in human terms, as far as that is possible. It must be a definition that will give a deeper understanding of the Church's actual, fundamental constitution, and show more clearly her diversified, salvific mission.

The theological doctrine is susceptible of magnificent development clearly deserving of the attentive consideration of our separated brothers. It is Our ardent hope that this development will make their path toward common agreement much easier.

The first among the many different questions to be dealt with by the Council is one which pertains directly to you as bishops of God's Church, and We have no hesitation in admitting that We await this discussion with eager anticipation and genuine confidence. The doctrine to which We are referring is that of the episcopate, its functions and its relation to Peter. Indeed, this doctrine ought to be gone into very thoroughly (while at the same time we hold safe the dogmatic pronouncements of the First Vatican Council concerning the Roman Pontiff). For us personally it will provide doctrinal and practical standards for the exercise of Our apostolic office. This universal office has been endowed by Christ, as you know, with the fullness and sufficiency of power. Nevertheless, it can marshal to itself added support and assistance from an ever more effective and responsible collaboration (in ways and means to be determined) of Our beloved and revered brothers in the episcopate.

After the elucidation of this doctrine, consideration will have to be given to the composition of Christ's visible and mystical body, the pilgrim, militant Church on earth: priests, religious, the faithful and our separated brothers, who are also called to full membership of the Church.

No one can fail to realize how supremely important this theological work of the Council will prove to be. It will, moreover, assist the Church's awareness of herself — of her power to bring forth light, joy and holiness. May God fulfill these hopes of Ours!

II

THE RENEWAL OF THE CHURCH

We entertained like hopes in regard to another main reason for this Council's summoning: the renewal of holy Church.

This, too, in Our opinion, must follow from our awareness of the relationship which unites the Church to Christ. We spoke just now of the Church looking upon Christ to discern in Him her true likeness. If in so doing she discovers some shadow, some defect, some stain on her wedding garment, what should be her instinctive, vigorous reaction? Clearly no other course is open to her than to renew herself, to put herself to rights, and bring herself back into conformity with her divine model; for that is her primary duty.

We are reminded of the words which Jesus Christ uttered in his priestly prayer on the eve of his agony and death: "I dedicate myself for their sakes, that they too may be dedicated through the truth" (Jn 17:19).

The Second Ecumenical Council must, in Our view, accept and embrace that sure rule of life which is in accordance with the will of Christ. Only then, when the Church has completed this great work of her own interior sanctification, will she be able to show her face to the world and say: "Whoever has seen me, has seen the Father" (Jn 14:9).

In this respect an ecumenical council must be thought of as a new springtime, a reawakening of the mighty spiritual and moral forces which lie hidden, as it were, within the Church. The clear aim of this Council is to rejuvenate the Church's inner vitality and the regulations by which her canonical structure and liturgical forms are governed. It is a general synod which is striving to bring about in the Church an increase in that attractiveness and holiness which can only come from the imitation of Jesus Christ and mystical union with Him through the Holy Spirit.

The question of the Church's renewal is most certainly of great concern to this Council. But the expression of this desire must not be interpreted as an admission of guilt on the part of the Catholic Church of our day for having falsified the mind of her founder in a matter of grave moment. It is her feeling of real joy and gratitude at having proved loyal to Christ in matters of the highest importance which makes her all the more ready and anxious to correct those faults which derive from human frailty. Hence the renewal with which the Church is concerned must not be thought of as a repudiation of the present life of the Church or a break with essential and time-honored traditions. She shows her reverence for tradition by rejecting forms which are spurious or moribund, and by wishing to make them genuine and fruitful.

Was it not Christ Himself who said to His disciples: "I am the true vine, and it is my Father who tends it. The branch that yields no fruit in me, he cuts away; the branch that does yield fruit, he trims clean, so that it may yield more fruit" (Jn 15:1–2). These words of the Gospel are sufficient, and more than sufficient, to indicate the principal characteristics of that perfection to which the Church is now aspiring. The first concerns her inner vitality and the outward expression of this vitality. The living Church must respond to the living Christ. She lives by faith and love; nothing, therefore, must be neglected that can nourish that faith anew, and make it joyous and steadfast. Nothing must be neglected that can increase the power of a Christian upbringing and a Christian education to produce these effects. Undoubtedly the foundation of this renewal will be the exercise of a greater intensity, a greater dedication, in the study of divine truth. Secondly, a place of honor must be given to the law of charity. If we would have a Church capable of renewing herself and — more difficult still — of renewing the entire world around her, then we must aim to construct a *Church of love*. Charity, as we know, is the queen and mother of every other Christian virtue: humility, poverty, piety, self-sacrifice, courage in bearing witness to the faith, the love of justice, and every other force that activates the man reborn in Christ.

In this matter the Ecumenical Council will have to range over a wide field of subjects. Of these, one of the most noteworthy and matchless for the love that it engenders, is the sacred liturgy. You dealt with this at considerable length during the last session, and We trust that you will now reap the fruits of that discussion, and turn your minds to other topics with the same energy and enthusiasm. Time, it is feared, will not permit you to do justice to every subject that requires investigation. Some topics will have to be held over to a later session.

III

THE RESTORATION OF UNITY AMONG ALL CHRISTIANS

The third aim set the Council by Our predecessor John XXIII is one which in the realm of spiritual values must be considered of supreme importance. It concerns "other Christians," those, that is, who believe in Christ but whom we have not the happiness of numbering among ourselves in the perfect unity of Christ. This unity ought by rights to have been theirs by baptism. Of its very nature it is something which they desire most ardently, and only the one Catholic Church can offer it to them. The recent unity movement among separated Christian communions, which is growing stronger every day, makes two things plain: Christ's Church is one and should be one; and this mystic and visible unity cannot be achieved except by one faith, participation in the same sacraments, and the proper unifying effect of a single ecclesiastical regimen — allowing, however, for a variety of languages, traditional rites and customs, local prerogatives, different schools of spirituality, legitimate institutions, and freedom of choice in the activities of daily life.

What, then, is to be the feeling and the policy of this Council regarding the vast array of our separated brothers and the possibility of variety in unity? It is indeed an open question. The calling of this Council is unique in one respect: its aim is complete and universal "ecumenicity." That at least is what it desires. It is praying for it, preparing for it. Who knows? Today's ambition may tomorrow find fruition. The Council, while calling and counting its own those sheep who belong to Christ's fold in the fullest and truest sense, is opening the door and calling out in eager expectation to the many sheep of Christ who are not at present within the one fold. The purpose of this Council, therefore, is to extend an invitation, and to look forward with expectancy to a more widespread, fraternal participation in its genuine "ecumenicity."

In all deference We address Ourself now to the representatives of the Christian denominations separated from the Catholic Church, who have been sent to take part as observers in these solemn congregations.

We rejoice at being able to extend to them a cordial welcome. We thank them for their presence here.

Through them We send a message of fatherly, brotherly love to the respected Christian communities they represent.

Our voice falters and Our heart beats faster, as much for the marvelous hope and inexpressible consolation that their presence here brings Us, as for the deep sadness We feel at their prolonged separation.

If we are in any way to blame for this separation, we humbly beg God's forgiveness, and ask our brothers' pardon for any injuries they feel they have sustained from us. For our part, we willingly forgive whatever injuries the Catholic Church has suffered, and forget the grief she has endured, as a result of the long years of dissension and separation.

May our heavenly Father be pleased to accept this avowal of ours, and give to all of us true, brotherly peace.

In the very nature of the case the problems which remain between us are serious and complex. These must be examined and dealt with; a solution must be found. We, for Our part, would wish that this could come about at once "in the charity of Christ which urges us." But We realize that for these problems to be dealt with satisfactorily, many conditions are required which have so far not fully materialized. But We are not averse to waiting patiently for the happy day when perfect reconciliation will be received at last.

Meanwhile, We wish to lay before the observers here certain principles relating to Our attitude toward reunion with our separated brothers, so that they may pass them on to their respective Christian communities. May Our voice also reach those other separated yet revered Christian communities who did not accept Our invitation to be present, without prejudice to either side, at this Council. We believe these points are already well known, but it will be useful to repeat them here.

What We have to say is spoken in friendship and complete sincerity. We are not trying to lay a trap for them or to get the better of them in any worldly sense. We adhere most firmly and openly to our faith, as we must, for We fully believe it to be divine. But We are convinced that this is no obstacle to reaching that understanding with our separated brothers which We desire, for divine truth is a principle of unity, not of difference and separation. At all events, We do not wish to make of our faith an occasion for polemics.

Secondly, We have the highest regard and reverence for that ancient religious patrimony which we share in common with our separated brothers and which they have not only preserved but have also considerably enhanced. We certainly view with pleasure the studies engaged in by those who seek sincerely to improve relations between us by highlighting the treasures of truth and spirituality we have in common. We believe that they too are equally sincere, and genuinely desire to understand our own doctrine better and its logical development from the deposit of divine faith. We believe that they also are anxious to gain a fuller knowledge of our religious life and history.

Conscious though We are of the very serious difficulties which still come between us and that longed-for unity, We wish nevertheless to affirm that We place complete reliance on God. We will continue to pray to Him and do all We can to show clearer evidence of a truly Christian way of life and of fraternal charity. And even if events belie Our hope and expectation, We shall remember those consoling words of Christ: "What is impossible to man's powers is possible to God" (Lk 18:27).

IV

THE CHURCH'S DIALOGUE WITH MEN OF OUR OWN DAY

The final aim of the Council is to bridge the gulf between ourselves and contemporary society. It is a remarkable fact that the Church, although distinct and set apart from the world around her — in virtue of that continual inner vitality which she derives from the Holy Spirit — is at the same time the lifegiving leaven of human society and its means of salvation. This fact reveals and confirms the missionary task which she has to perform. It is her most important duty: to show keenness and enthusiasm in obeying her command to preach the Gospel to mankind of every condition.

But you, dearest brothers, have already experienced this marvelous circumstance. At the very beginning of the first session, inspired by John XXIII's inaugural speech, you immediately made your presence felt beyond the walls of this hall of assembly in the clear message of greeting, fraternity and hope you sent out to the whole world. It was an unprecedented and wonderful gesture. It was as though the gift of prophecy given to the Church had suddenly become vocal. Just as St. Peter on the day of Pentecost was impelled to speak out to the people without an instant's delay, so you too felt the immediate desire to deal, not with your own concerns, but with those of the whole human family. You wished to speak, not just among yourselves, but to all mankind.

This shows, dearest brothers, that charity is indeed the special mark of this Council — a charity that is strong and all embracing; a charity that thinks of others rather than of itself; the universal charity of Christ!

This charity sustains Us now in the face of a contemporary scene which tends to inspire fear rather than consolation, sorrow rather than joy, and to incline us more to obviate risks and condemn errors than to rely on trust and friendship.

We have to face facts. We cannot conceal the wound that for a variety of reasons has been inflicted even on this universal Synod. Are We so blind as not to be able to see the many vacant places in this assembly? Where are our brothers from those nations which are warring on the Church? What is the state of religion there? What of Our sacred Hierarchy, Our religious men and women, Our countless children subjected to fear, persecution, misery and oppression because of their staunch loyalty to Christ and to His Church? What We know about their condition is bad enough; what We are not allowed to know only increases Our fears. We are overwhelmed with sadness at the thought of their sufferings. We grieve to see how in certain countries religious liberty and other fundamental human rights are being crushed by principles and policies characterized by their political, racial and religious intolerance. We grieve at the many injustices that are still inflicted in some countries on people who wish to profess their religion openly and honestly. But in deploring these evils We have no desire to resort to abuse. Rather We use once again the language of sincere exhortation, appealing to the humanity of those responsible, and begging them at long last to end their groundless hostility to the Catholic religion. Let them not think of Catholics as enemies and traitors, but rather as honest and industrious citizens of the nations to which they belong. We take this opportunity of sending Our warmest greetings to those Catholics who are suffering for their faith, and We pray God to console them in their distress.

Nor does Our sadness end here, for We are sick at heart at the sight of the many other evils affecting the human family. The greatest of these is atheism which, having engulfed a section of human society, is overthrowing the social order and step by step obliterating from men's minds the true notion of this order. While the light of natural sciences is increasing, darkness, alas, is beginning to spread over the science of God, and hence over the true science of man. While scientific progress is marvelously perfecting every kind of instrument for man's use, his heart is tormented more and more each day by loneliness, sadness and despair.

There is much more We should say about the complex and — for many reasons — bitter problems affecting the men of our day; but time will not permit. Today, as We have said, Our heart burns with that same charity with which the Church in Council is aglow. We look with the utmost good will on this age of ours and its interplay of varied and contrasting forces, and We long most ardently to hand on to the men of our day that message of love, salvation and hope which Christ brought into the world. For "when God sent his Son into the world, it was not to reject the world, but so that the world might find salvation through him" (Jn 3:17).

The world will surely realize that the Church looks upon it with profound understanding, with sincere admiration, and with the sincere intention not of mastering it, but of serving it, not of despising it but of increasing its dignity, not of condemning it but of bringing it comfort and salvation.

In this Council from which a window opens out upon the whole world, the Church looks with especial solicitude on certain groups of men: on the poor, the needy and distressed, the starving, the suffering, the imprisoned. She has a special concern for that part of the human race which is in misery and sorrow, for she knows that these men are hers by the very law of the Gospel. Joyfully, therefore, she addresses to them the words of her Lord: "Come to me, all of you" (Mt 11:28).

The Church also casts her eyes on men of learning, in literature, science and the arts. These too she holds in the highest esteem. With the utmost enthusiasm she welcomes their experiments, endorses the efforts of their genius, safeguards their liberty, and opens to their feverish and tormented spirits the gateway to the supernatural world of the divine Word and divine grace.

She has eyes too for working men, for their personal dignity and the dignity of their work, their legitimate demands, their urgent need, even in these days, to improve their social condition and progress spiritually. They have a task to perform, but it must be done properly and in a Christian spirit: it is to found a new order in which all men are free and acknowledge each other as brothers. Their mother and teacher, the Church, is solidly with them.

She turns her eyes to the rulers of nations. Often enough she has had to appeal to them with serious words of warning; today her words are full of encouragement and confidence. Take heart, you who guide the destinies of nations. Today you are in a position to supply the good things your people need: food, culture, order, the dignity that belongs to free citizens living together in peace. But to do so you must fully understand man's nature, and only Christian wisdom can teach you this. Your concerted efforts, founded on justice and love, can win for mankind the greatest of all blessings, that peace for which the world is thirsting, and which the Church protects and promotes with all her strength. Thus can you make of humanity a single city. May God be with you!

The Catholic Church looks further still, beyond the confines of the Christian family. For how can she set limits to her love if she would take as her model the love of God the Father who rains down His blessing on all men alike, and who so loved the world as to give His only-begotten Son to redeem it. She looks, then, beyond her own sphere, and regards those other religions which preserve the awareness and the conception of the one supreme, transcendent God, creator and sustainer, worshipping Him with acts of sincere devotion, and basing their moral and social life on these beliefs and practices.

The Catholic religion cannot ignore these other religions. Though it pains her to see the gaps, the insufficiencies and errors in their religious thinking, she hastens to assure them of her due regard for everything they have which is true and good and human. She would have them know that, as the defender of God's laws among men, she stands in the forefront of the fight to preserve religion and the worship of God in the world.

And finally the Church turns her eyes to other vast fields of human endeavor: the new generation of young people who are growing up fired with zest for life and the desire to outstrip the past; the new nations claiming recognition for their rights; countless men who toil in solitude surrounded by the turmoil of a human society which has no answer to their problems. To each and all the Church speaks words of hope, bringing them the light of truth, of life, and of salvation. For it is God's will "that all men should be saved, and be led to recognize the truth" (1 Tm 2:4).

We, dearest brothers, are the ministers of salvation, and our task is a heavy though a noble one. We are gathered here together in this solemn session to help us to perform it more worthily. May the sure, fraternal harmony of our spirits be our guidance and our strength. May our fellowship with the Church in Heaven stand us in good stead: those saints who are specially venerated in your various dioceses and religious orders, all angels and saints, especially Saints Peter and Paul, St. John the Baptist, and above all St.

Joseph, proclaimed the patron of this Council. May the most blessed Virgin Mary assist us who earnestly invoke her strong and motherly protection. And, under Christ's leadership, may all things redound to the glory of God in honor of the most holy Trinity, whose blessing We confidently bestow upon you all, in the name of the Father and of the Son and of the Holy Ghost.

(*At the end of his allocution, the Holy Father spoke the following words in Greek.*)

We are directing our cordial greetings to the Christians of the Eastern tradition, too, in the Greek tongue which was the language of the early ecumenical councils, of the great Fathers and Doctors of the Church: Basil the Great, Gregory of Nyssa, Gregory Nazianzen, John Chrysostom, Cyril of Alexandria, John Damascene and of so many others who enlightened the whole world and are the glory of Christian thought.

Brothers of the Holy Churches of the East: Let us pray and let us work, with faith and love, for the glory of God and for the spread of His Kingdom!

(*The Holy Father then spoke the following in Russian.*)

We also greet the Christians of the Slavic nations and We express to them Our desire to pray and to work for the glory of God and for the spread of His kingdom in faith and in love.